Miracle on Royal Place

The First 25 Years

ALASKA
CHRISTIAN
COLLEGE

Keith Hamilton

Table of Contents

Introduction

Since early 2000, I have been writing the story of Alaska Christian College in nearly a dozen hand-written journals that have been transcribed into a 400-page file. Instead of having you read my journals, I decided it was best to write the story of ACC using my journals as the basis for the book, in addition to recent interviews with the many people who have formed ACC's story of miracles.

While much of the book demonstrates sincere love and support from the Evangelical Covenant Church denomination and the Alaska Conference, I wish to honor and thank the many independent churches and mission-hearted denominations that have also walked this journey with us, all believing in Christian higher education and the impact it has on the age group and Indigenous students we serve.

I also want to thank my friend Bob Smietana, from Religion News Service and former Covenant writer, who has worked alongside Denise Mund, ACC volunteer archivist, to transcribe the first 25 years of this incredible ministry into our 25th anniversary book. It is my hope that sometime in the future, the full 25 plus years of my journals will be made public to tell much more of the story, since not everything could be written in this book. There is so much more to share of the goodness of God than these pages can tell. It is hard remembering so many people and details over the years but onward we must go with the telling of our story, and God's story.

God showed up in Soldotna! Since the beginning of its ministry in 2000, Alaska Christian College has been a story of God's *miracles* in the lives of our students, the properties and buildings, and the many who have served here—both volunteer and employed. These stories are the demonstration of God moving mightily in the State of Alaska to create an amazing ministry from its very simple beginnings. ACC has become a fully accredited college, serving Alaska's best Indigenous students seeking a degree in Christian higher education and the life-changing education only offered by Alaska Christian College. This book of stories shows through word and pictures the amazing provision of God and the story that continues as you read each miraculous event. Walk with us through God's story of how He has built this safe, beautiful, and Spirit-driven campus to the glory of God and Alaska's Indigenous students (and others who joined us along the way).

Many have asked me over the years how this was my vision to plant a Native-focused college in Alaska. I always respond that it wasn't my vision, but that of the Evangelical Covenant Church of Alaska that planted the vision and asked me to implement their vision. And while the ministry has changed over the years, the vision has remained steadfast. My prayer is that every young person (and others) throughout Alaska (and Outside–what Alaskans say when anyone is leaving the state) will find their way to ACC so that our campus is busting-out with students meeting Christ, being formed as disciples, educated to serve their communities, and healed from past wounds and hurts. This has always been our mission and vision.

From the most humble beginnings of this college, that has always fought above its weight class, I say to God be the glory, great things *He* has done!

Quyana and Taikuu,
Rev. Dr. Keith J. Hamilton
Founding President, Alaska Christian College
Summer 2025

Foreword

In January of 1994, I was the Field Director of the Evangelical Covenant Church of Alaska and processing a severe disappointment. I was in Chicago, having attended some Covenant church meetings, and decided to take a three-day prayer retreat, one that I committed to God would be kept in quiet. During this time (though I think I broke my vow of silence after about two hours), God opened my ears long enough to speak something to me. I've learned to hold myself suspect when I believe God is impressing something on me. That said, there have been a handful of times when I believe God was speaking very clearly. This was one of those times.

Three specific actions were impressed on me. I do not imply any kind of spiritual superstardom in that I did each of them. The stories of the other two are for another day, and I won't mention them here. The third was to do all I could to help start a residential school for college-age students from Alaska. I sat down and wrote up somewhere between a five-to-eight page plan for the launching of what would become Alaska Christian College.

Let me tell you about day one of acting on the vision. In retrospect, I'm not sure how much was zealous naiveté and how much was conviction. I changed my ticket, and instead of flying back directly to Alaska, I flew instead to Portland, Oregon. I'd recently learned that across the river in Vancouver, Washington, was a nonprofit entity, the M. J. Murdock Charitable Trust, that was interested in partnering with people with good plans to do good in Alaska. Usually one makes an appointment with an officer of such an organization months ahead; it's wise to even wear a clean-pressed suit. I showed up in my Sorrels, jeans, and a flannel shirt, in the state of dishevelment that has historically made my wife concerned any time I left the house. It so happened that the executive director of the Murdock Trust, Dr. Steven Moore, was in on his day off and agreed to meet me for five minutes. We ended up talking for over an hour, and he told me to come back when I actually had something of substance to show him. That said, it was clear that his heart was beating with what was in my heart. (Murdock would go on to contribute millions and provide invaluable mentoring and accountability.) I mention it here because of the reality of Ephesians 2:10. "We are God's workmanship, created in Christ Jesus to do good works, which He has prepared in advance for us to do." The story of ACC from that day until now has been written by God as He prepared the way.

At that time, in my late 30s, I realized that I had witnessed a variety of settings in which Christians were coming to faith and flourishing in their lives and service. A few years prior, I had begun to ask myself what each of these had in common. A phrase, "compelling Christian community," pulled it together: Christian, in that the living Christ, loved and sent by the Father, and continuing to be made known by the Holy Spirit, is at the center; community, reflecting both the character of the Trinity and God's purpose for His people and the world. We live in a relationship-centered universe. Life finds its purpose and power in loving relationship with God, others, and relational appreciation for all He has created. When Christ is truly at the center of a community, and His people know they are loved incomprehensibly by Him, and they pursue a life claiming their birthright to love each other and to love the world without measure or reservation, the Spirit of Christ is unleashed. In such a community, the place where faith is grown is the same place where healing, self-awareness, forgiveness, kindness, and resilience are grown. Such Christian communities are compelling for those within them and those they touch. It was the hope that Alaska Christian College would be a place where young people living and studying in community would be transformed by authentically living in relationship with God and others: that it would be a compelling Christian community.

It is important to understand that at this point we had no program, no people to lead the program, and no place to live out this vision. Prior to jumping right in, it made sense to run a pilot of what this community might look like. With that in mind, the plan in the binder included a 100-day-long pilot program. Of course, we had no money! And running any kind of program does require some financial resources. The hope was to put together some Christian leaders with a handful of promising students for 100 days, do some training in Biblical studies, provide service outlets, and get a recruiting engine ignited for the eventual residential program. Hearing about Franklin Graham's recent purchase of a turboprop Mitsubishi, which was housed in Soldotna, I thought this could be the perfect instrument to enable this to happen. Presumptuously, I needed the plane for free. Graham's ministry, Samaritan's Purse, generously rose to the occasion to accommodate our shoestring budget. For the next few months, their aircraft carried our students from one location, mostly western Alaskan villages, to another. Pastors and other mentors taught the little band of six students; the students shared in local schools, and served in various other meaningful ways.

It's encouraging to recollect that the entire budget for this program was $10,000. The plan was to rely primarily on the generosity of the villages of Alaska to feed and house the students, but still we needed the $10,000. At the Covenant Church's denomination annual meeting, I was seated next to a kindly retired couple. As we visited, I shared my hope to get the pilot program off the ground (pun intended). The next morning, they informed me that they had transferred a bit more than $5,000 worth of stock to the Covenant Church of Alaska for this program. Knowing nothing about stocks, the following day, I bought, for the first time in my life, a copy of the *Wall Street Journal* and looked up the stock. In the previous 24 hours, it had doubled! We had our $10,000! I was that much more convinced that God wanted this thing to happen. A MIRACLE!

It's important to note that while friendships grew, the students and volunteer leaders also at times drove each other crazy. German pastor and theologian Dietrich Bonhoeffer taught that one needs to work through disillusionment to experience true community. Bonhoeffer teaches that our ideal of the Christian life and relationships are idolatry; the real is what happens in the actual non-idealized world with all of its challenges and heartaches, real people with our persistent faults living with the real God. The compelling Christian community is not built on a mountain top. It persists through the rubble of sin, broken relationships, mistakes, seeking forgiveness, offering forgiveness, and the sweet freedom of reconciliation. The 25 years of ACC have been remade and refreshed multiple times in this way of the Spirit.

While I was heavily involved in the first year of ACC, my contribution to the story is primarily before the wonderful 25-year journey of the college we are celebrating. I'll only add that getting the right people always puts you well onto a path of fruitfulness. Mark Hill, Curtis Ivanoff, Jeff Siemers, and Keith Hamilton were the four people I believed could get this off the ground. I even told the Murdock people on day one about each of these individuals, saying, if they responded with a yes, I'd be back. Mark is now serving as a Major in the U.S. Air Force as a chaplain. Curtis became the first Native superintendent of the Alaska Conference of the Covenant Church. Jeff serves as the executive vice president of ACC and provost and has been there almost all of its history. Keith, of course, is the founding and only president ACC has known. Keith's wife, Debbie, founded the New Hope Counseling Center on campus, which has ministered wholeness and healing to students, staff, and the wider Kenai Peninsula community. I am grateful to them, and all the staff, volunteers, and students who have lived out the ACC vision. I am especially appreciative and a bit in awe of Keith and Jeff, who through the strength, wisdom, and tenacity God has given them, serve until this very day.

Your Brother and Friend,
Paul V. Wilson
Meridian, Idaho

Dedication

Since this may be the only time I write a book, I absolutely need to give my deepest thanks and incredible love to my wife, Debbie, who has walked and ministered alongside me all these 25 years and more. Her role at New Hope Counseling Center and being an über supportive spouse and mom has made this miracle on Royal Place more possible.

Throughout all the journey from when they were five, three, and one, I am indebted to our three grown children, Brad, Chris, and Megan, who have traveled the path with us all of these first 25 years. I am grateful to them for allowing Debbie and me to pursue the greatest adventure of our lives together as one family on mission. To my loving and supportive family, I dedicate this book.

In Memoriam

With over 900 students having walked through ACC's doors since its inception in 2000/2001, we honor and remember the many students who have passed. Our hope is that they have been made anew by the hope of eternal life that faith in Jesus promises to those who trust Him.

In addition, we remember the many volunteers who played crucial roles in the building and programming of the campus who have passed. They are too numerous to mention here, but some may be found in the pages ahead.

We fondly remember our Board of Trustees chair, Rev. Nathan Toots, who capably led us in our early years, and his passing. Peace to his memory as well as George Mueller and Tom Mute, Trustees.

Finally, we remember and honor staff members who have passed since the college opened its doors: Bob and Phyllis Mickelson (Clear Lake, Washington), Millie Mehrkens (Red Wing, Minnesota), and Jan Eppard (Red Wing, Minnesota).

"Being confident of this, that He who began a good work in you will carry it on to completion until the day of Christ Jesus." (Phil. 1:6)

1

In the spring of 2000, Rev. Keith Hamilton, the Associate Pastor to Youth at Arvada Covenant Church near Denver, received a visit from an old friend. On the Sunday after Easter, Mossai Sanguma—his former seminary classmate and then-president of the Evangelical Covenant Church in the Democratic Republic of Congo—was the guest preacher, delivering a sermon on mission.

As the service concluded, the congregation began singing "I, the Lord of Sea and Sky," a hymn often associated with missionary work. The song's refrain echoes Isaiah 6, where God asks, "Whom shall I send? Who will go for us?" Isaiah responds, "Here I am, send me." The hymn echoes this sentiment:

Here I am, Lord. Is it I, Lord?
I have heard you calling in the night.
I will go, Lord, if you lead me,
I will hold your people in my heart.

Seated in the pews, Keith and his wife, Debbie, felt a deep stirring. For years, they had led short-term mission trips to Mexico, Spain, Canada, Ecuador, and Alaska, giving young people the chance to serve and experience different cultures. After two decades in youth ministry, they sensed that God was calling them toward something new.

For months, they had been discussing what that change might be. Keith Hamilton had been invited to interview for the Executive Director role at Covenant Bible College (CBC), which was preparing to launch a new campus in Ecuador. The Hamiltons felt sure that a shift was coming.

They didn't know what lay ahead, but they were ready to follow wherever God led. "That song has always moved us," Debbie later recalled. "By the end, we were both in tears—just a heartfelt desire to be available."

Their openness to change made them consider the possibility of moving to Ecuador with CBC. Rev. Neil Josephson, the school's president, had asked Keith to pray about leading the project. While there were no guarantees—other candidates were also being considered—the opportunity seemed promising.

"The Lord was already planting seeds in our hearts that something next was coming and was priming us," Debbie would recall. "We just didn't know what that next was."

During a car ride, Keith and Debbie began talking about their dreams for the future and what might be possible. Both had administrative and people skills and wanted to help young people grow in their faith—a passion honed over years in youth ministry. Both, as well, were open to working in a cross-cultural setting. Keith had always prayed that if God called him to serve anywhere in the world, it would be best to include mission, youth ministry, and discipleship. He said, "I will go anywhere in the world, Lord, if I can be used in these three specific areas, especially Hawaii."

As they were considering what might come next, Keith received a call from Rev. Paul Wilson, who was then the leader of Evangelical Covenant Church's (ECCAK) work in Alaska. Church leaders there had been thinking about starting a year-long discipleship college, modeled along the lines of CBC, in Alaska, and wanted to know if he might be interested in leading the project.

He was. Keith had already spent time in western Alaska, making friends with pastors and other leaders there—and building the kind of network and trust that would be needed in the college's early days. The Hamiltons were also familiar with CBC's model—as Keith had taught classes at the school in Canada and had helped get the school's Colorado campus off the ground and served as its vice chair, hoping that that experience might prove useful for the kind of work that Wilson was talking about.

They also had some familiarity with the challenges facing young people in Alaska—and knew that starting ACC would be about more than just education— the students would need social, emotional, and spiritual support. The school would need the kind of entrepreneurial spirit the Hamiltons had—but specifically the skills that Debbie had as a licensed counselor. Starting the school would also mean starting a counseling ministry from scratch—with no funding and few resources, something the Hamilton's felt they might be able to do.

The proposed project seemed a good fit. Ironically, the Hamiltons had already played a small role in helping the idea of Alaska Christian College get started. A year earlier, about the time that the Hamiltons had begun talking with CBC, they received a visit from a longtime friend and the founder of Covenant Youth of Alaska, a statewide youth ministry in the Evangelical Covenant Church of Alaska better known by the acronym CYAK.

Byron Bruckner was in Colorado to visit Arvada Covenant Church, hoping to raise funds for a new initiative called Alaska Leadership College. The idea, Bruckner explained, was to start a program to help young Alaska Native adults make the transition from high school to college—by teaching classes as well as doing service projects. Bruckner was hoping to raise about $10,000 for the project. Since Arvada Covenant had long been supportive of youth work in Alaska, he hoped the church might get on board with this new project.

Hamilton supported the idea and recommended it to Arvada Covenant's mission board. The two had been in Alaska the previous year and had visited the Lazy Mountain campus of Interact Ministries in Palmer, Alaska, which had once been the site of a children's home and, later, a Bible college. Knowing the needs of students in Alaska, the two had talked about whether or not the Covenant could start a Bible college of its own someday in Alaska—an idea that had been long under discussion among church leaders in that state.

For several years, Bruckner and other leaders in CYAK, had been pondering a similar idea. The Alaska Covenant had had a long interest in education and youth ministry in Alaska, and was mentioned in discussions at summer Bible camps and church gatherings, and the idea had been percolating. Bruckner's trip to Arvada was an early step in bringing those ideas to life.

The timing was fortuitous. Arvada Covenant was planning to sell a parsonage the church owned and wanted to use some of the funds for missions. The church's mission board decided the new leadership project in Alaska was a good option and eventually, $10,000 from the parsonage sale was given to the church in Alaska to get the project off the ground. A MIRACLE!

"I recommended this project, never knowing that someday I would be its first president," Hamilton would later write.

Those funds would indeed be used for the pilot project called "Alaska Leadership College," a three-month traveling ministry led by CYAK leaders, including Jeff Siemers, who was to later join the launch team for ACC.

"Things like this don't come out of nothing," Bruckner said. In a 2024 interview, he pointed back to the development of Covenant High School, a Covenant Church–operated high school, which had been open from the 1950s to the mid-1980s. When that school started, said Bruckner, Westernization was coming to the western part of Alaska—especially with statehood looming on the horizon. (Alaska, which was purchased from Russia in the 1860s, became the 49th state in 1959.) At that time, missionaries and church leaders were asking the question, "What do we need to do to prepare for the future?" Asking that question, said Bruckner, led to the founding of Covenant High School.

"The thinking at that time was that we need a high school because we need to catch the students when they're young and connect with them," Bruckner said.

Church leaders hoped the high school would help young Alaska Native people have control over their futures—to be proactive, rather than reacting to the changes around them. To do that, Bruckner said, the school tried to offer the highest quality education possible. The school also had a spiritual purpose—providing community and spiritual formation for students.

That school had a long legacy, said Bruckner. "You have a lot of leaders that have come out of Covenant High School, even to this day," he said.

Rev. Paul Wilson, who was the field director for the Covenant's work in Alaska when the idea of ACC was first developed, recalled attending a reunion for graduates of Covenant High School not long after arriving in the state—and being struck by how important that school had been for the life of the church in Alaska.

Rev. Curtis Ivanoff, who became one of the ACC start-up leaders, recounted in a history of Covenant High, that the school, which was founded in 1954, offered "a quality education as well as a concern for the spiritual lives of students." The idea was to provide secondary education for promising students and to build future leaders among Alaska Native Christians, according to the principles that guided the school's founding. The school, which closed in 1985, had also sought to prepare students both academically and spiritually for a rapidly changing world—and to empower them with the tools needed to help shape that world.

That included teaching classes in English, rather than Native languages. Al White, who taught industrial arts at the school in its early days, described that decision this way, in a 2008 interview with Ivanoff, "English is coming and is overtaking the local languages," he said, recounting a conversation about teaching in English. "It's like a steamroller that is coming and either the steamroller is going to crush people in its way or there will be people on the steamroller driving it. I would rather have students driving the steamroller."

The work of CYAK, Wilson said in a 2023 interview, was a precursor to the founding of ACC and set the tone for the school's culture of tight-knit and supportive Christian community. The ministry provided spiritual guidance and care for students while creating a network of new leaders. Several of the staff who became part of the school's founding got their initial exposure to ministry from working with young people.

"We saw you can have two things," Wilson said. "You're serving students, but you are (also) developing a community of leaders who would be friends."

"Over time," Wilson added, "good things would happen from that."

CYAK began in the 1990s to fill some of the void left when Covenant High School closed in 1985. When Covenant High opened, it was one of the few high schools serving Alaska Native teenagers in rural villages, as few small communities had public high schools. That changed in 1975, with the famed Molly Hootch case—where a young Alaska Native woman sued the State of Alaska for failing to provide public education to high school-aged students in Native villages. The State began public high school options for village students after the Alaska Supreme Court ruled in her favor in 1976, meaning that the Alaska Department of Education agreed to build local high schools in rural villages with at least 25 students.

Ministry leaders in Alaska felt the absence of Covenant High School, which provided a cadre of youth with spiritual formation and community building in Unalakleet. Unalakleet was also home to the Covenant Bible Camp, another important component to reaching young people from rural Alaska.

"That was a real discouragement when the doors had to close at Covenant High because that was also a gathering spot in a place of spiritual formation and discipleship for students," said Bruckner.

By the 1990s, church leaders in Alaska had begun to look for new ways to serve young people in the church. Because many of the Covenant congregations were small, few could afford to have youth pastors on staff. Consequently, they began pooling their resources together for projects like Covenant Bible Camp.

Bruckner, who was born in Nome and grew up in a missionary family—his dad had initially come to Alaska as a pilot, and his mom was a nurse—returned home after college and hoped to get involved in youth ministry. He and other leaders began to work on the model for what would become CYAK.

Like ACC, CYAK started from humble beginnings. Bruckner recalled at the time, the entire budget for Covenant fieldwork in Alaska was about $120,000—which was barely enough to keep things running, let alone to start a statewide youth ministry.

"When I first went to the Alaska Covenant field leaders and shared the idea, they said, 'Well, that's a wonderful concept and idea, but we have no money,'" Bruckner said.

A child of missionaries, Bruckner knew what it was like to start a ministry on a shoestring. And he had connections in the broader Covenant world—many of whom he knew might be willing to support CYAK, if Bruckner and other leaders could share the vision of what they envisioned for ministering to young people in Alaska. Armed with some fresh salmon for fundraising dinners and a dream to plant this ministry, Bruckner headed to the lower 48 to visit Covenant churches where he shared the story of youth work in Alaska.

One of the first places he visited was Arvada Covenant Church, where Rev. Keith Hamilton was then the youth pastor. The two became friends and bonded over their shared love for youth work and missions. That friendship led to Hamilton bringing his youth groups to Alaska, where he built friendships with Covenanters there. On a return visit, Bruckner recalled bringing along Ivanoff, introducing him to Hamilton and other Covenant leaders.

CYAK, in some ways, became a kind of proof of concept for the launch of Alaska Christian College. Both were starting to meet a need in the Alaska church and were built on faith and friendship—and the desire to empower young people in the church.

During the early years of CYAK, Bruckner traveled the state looking for leaders, in particular young adults, who could get involved in youth ministry. He'd often talk to older church members but had a harder time finding younger adults. Then he recalled someone asking him, "Have you met Curtis Ivanoff?"

At the time, Ivanoff was a college student at the University of Oklahoma, where he'd gone after graduating from high school in Alaska.

"I called him, and I said, 'Tell me your story. Let's connect,'" Bruckner said.

When Ivanoff and his wife, Kristi, moved back to Alaska, where Curtis worked as a public school math teacher in both Noorvik then Unalakleet, they both dove into youth ministry as volunteers in Unalakleet. Things went well enough that Wilson and Bruckner began to look for ways to bring Ivanoff into full-time pastoral ministry.

As CYAK grew, a number of other key leaders came on board, many of them who'd eventually be part of the start-up team for ACC or played a role in the school's development. Among them, John Hege, a former Youth for Christ staffer from Montana, moved to Alaska and began working as a youth pastor in Shaktoolik, a village on the Norton Sound. Other leaders arrived as well, such as Mark Hill and Steve Peterson. Mark had been serving in rural Alaska as a youth leader and broadcaster with the Alaska Covenant Church's radio station in Nome, KICY. He would soon become ACC's second hire in the area of recruitment and enrollment. Peterson became a youth pastor in Anchorage at First Covenant Church and later became a longtime public school teacher.

"We were really focusing on camp, and then we were encouraging kids to go off to Covenant Bible College—and we began to think, if there was a discipleship school for students (in Alaska), that would be a much better experience for them," Bruckner recalled.

Eventually, he said, CYAK was sending 8 to 10 students a year to Covenant Bible College. At the same time, Hamilton continued to bring young people to Alaska on mission trips.

"Those two lines converged," said Bruckner, speaking of the genesis of a Covenant college in Alaska, with Hamilton as a key leader.

In the mid-1990s, Bruckner and his wife moved to Fairbanks to work with Covenant young people who were studying at the University of Alaska. The move came out of some strategic planning with Paul Wilson, who had arrived on the scene as the new regional field director for the Covenant Church of Alaska. They hoped to extend the work CYAK was doing with junior high and high school students to young adults in college.

The idea was to work with students from ages 12 to 25, during key formative years of their lives. "We needed to help them continue to grow in their faith and make sure they are on solid ground spiritually," Bruckner said.

Looking back, that experience in Fairbanks also proved to be a testing ground for an intentional Christian community for Alaska Native students at the university. Several students ended up living with the Bruckners—who served as their mentors, helping students learn to live out their faith one day at a time, in the nitty-gritty details of life.

Alongside this on-the-ground ministry, Covenant leaders working with young people were also making their way through a strategic planning process. During that process, CYAK leaders began to investigate the possibility of starting a school of discipleship similar to Covenant Bible College in Prince Albert, Saskatchewan, Canada.

The first step, said Bruckner, was to invite CBC staff to speak at Bible camp and other CYAK events and to start building relationships between the school and Covenant churches in Alaska. At the time CBC was also expanding, which led to some discussion about the possibility of starting another campus of the school in Alaska. But those talks ended up stalling out. CBC had already started a campus in Colorado in 1998 and plans were underway for another campus in Ecuador in 2000. CBC Canada Conference leadership believed the timing was just not right for an Alaska campus for CBC.

Still, Bruckner, Wilson, and other leaders felt a need to move forward.

"During that strategic planning time, we said, 'Okay we are ready—we need this to happen,'" said Bruckner, recalling conversations in the late 1990s. "Part of that motivation was that we had students in the pipeline."

"After that strategic planning time, it was clear we wanted to try to do this discipleship school," said Bruckner.

If the school were to be in Alaska, leaders figured they'd have 15 to 20 students who would likely choose the school, rather than going to Canada or Colorado. Bruckner and other leaders also knew they had the relationships in place and the potential supporters who could make the school a success.

Recently, the Superintendent of the Alaska Conference of the Evangelical Covenant Church, Curtis Ivanoff, sat down for an interview about his time at ACC in the fall of 2024 as one of the founding ACC team members. Ivanoff had just returned from meetings with pastors, which capped a busy season filled with meetings and funerals.

Ivanoff recalled having early conversations about starting a Bible college in the mid-1990s, about the time when CBC was expanding its ministry. CBC, which started in Saskatchewan during the 1940s, was experiencing a season of growing enrollment, prompting a move from Prince Albert to Strathmore, Alberta in 1996.

Even with a new campus, the school could not keep up with demand. With a growing waiting list, the school began to look for places to expand. During that process, leaders of CYAK pitched CBC president Neil Josephson on the idea of CBC coming to Alaska. Ivanoff and his wife, Kristi, were there, along with other leaders like Byron Bruckner, John Hege, and then–Alaska Field Director Paul Wilson.

"We met after our young adult camps, which we called Vision," he said. "That was where we were dreaming of what could be."

CBC would eventually decide to look elsewhere for a new campus, expanding to Windsor, Colorado—with the help of the youth pastor named Keith Hamilton—in 1998, and two years later the third campus in Quito, Ecuador.

The time for a Bible college in Alaska was not yet ripe.

In an interview about the early days of ACC, Ivanoff also looked back to the closing of Covenant High School in Unalakleet, where he had attended his freshman year of high school. At that time, said Ivanoff, a verse from Ecclesiastes came to mind: "For everything, there is a season and a time for every matter under heaven."

It was a time of grief and gratefulness, said Ivanoff. People were thankful for the decades of ministry at the school and aware of what losing Covenant High meant by the church's ability to reach young people and empower them to take ownership of their futures. It was also a place where long-term relationships among future leaders in the church could be nurtured and developed.

"The school was a flagship and hub for youth ministry," said Ivanoff, who spent about a decade planting ACC along with the team before becoming leader of the Covenant denomination's work in Alaska.

While the vision for ACC began to solidify, one of the potential staffers for ACC, Jeff Siemers, was also being prepared for the work of ACC. Siemers was then working as a youth pastor in Hooper Bay, a larger village of 1,200 in western Alaska, south of Scammon Bay, with his longtime youth group friend, Marcus Reese. They were part of a growing community of youth pastors at village churches, who would be key to helping the college connect with young people in those communities. Mark Hill and Curtis Ivanoff, also key leaders in CYAK, would eventually join the ACC staff.

It was all part of having the right people in the right place at the right time.

Alaska Leadership College had successfully concluded its pilot project and even with the mission grant from Arvada Covenant Church, funds had run out. Those funds were needed mostly for the travel costs associated with the pilot program. Wilson had learned that Samaritan's Purse had a Mitsubishi MU2 airplane—which could accommodate about 10 people—available at their base in Soldotna, about a three-hour drive southwest of Anchorage. The plane was often used to transport volunteers and Samaritan's Purse staff—but the ministry had a break in its schedule and the plane was available for charter. Samaritan's Purse is an evangelical nonprofit with a base in Soldotna, Alaska, that ministers to Alaska Natives' physical needs, primarily through construction projects and wounded warriors-type programs.

For $10,000, Wilson made a deal to use the plane for a three-month-long pilot project, to demonstrate the feasibility of the college's program.

"The idea was, we'll show you what we are doing," said Wilson.

Along with testing the concept of the college, the pilot project would also provide visibility for the leadership college, which until that point had been little known outside church leaders.

"The thought was, this was going to do a few things," said Wilson. "One is, we are going to get a little experience of what it is going to be like with the students. Two, it is going to be advertising for the college."

The pilot project proved essential to getting the college off the ground. Bruckner recalled that in the late 1990s, the memory of closing Covenant High School was still on the mind of Covenant leaders, especially those at the denominational level. At the time, the Alaska region/field was still a mission field of the denomination and had close ties to what was then known as the Department of Church Growth and Evangelism, a division of the Evangelical Covenant Church denomination, where ACC would receive its oversight in the initial years.

There was denominational concern about starting another school, said Bruckner, because of the possibility that it might fail.

Wilson also wanted the school to focus on relationships and discipleship—and not get caught up in trying to acquire a building, at least at the start. He had in mind more of a mission trip–style approach, with a group of students traveling from village to village, doing service projects, and holding classes at churches.

While that worked for the pilot project, that kind of model proved unworkable for the long haul.

"The conclusion was, we need to have a residential site," he said. "It was too hard to live out of a suitcase and try to run a discipleship program on the fly and in the air all the time," Bruckner said. The pilot project did, however, give the school the momentum it needed to get off the ground. People saw the need and saw that the project would work."

Still, the success of that three-month project gave a boost of confidence to leaders that they were on the right track. Some of the details of the project had been lost or obscured as time passed. Ivanoff recalled the pilot project included five Alaska Native students as well as a young Indigenous woman from Siberia—who traveled from village to village for three months, taking classes and doing service projects. As mentioned earlier, Jeff Siemers, who would go on to be one of the initial staff members at ACC, led this small group of students in the pilot program.

Del Pease, a staffer from CBC, taught some of the classes, as well as Wilson and other local leaders. Ivanoff, a former public school teacher and youth leader who had transitioned to full-time ministry, did some teaching while the group was in Nome. He also met up with them at several youth events that year.

"I taught some Russian," he said. "Because at that time, the Iron Curtain had fallen and there was a lot of ministry partnership across the ocean to Russia that was going on." One of the students, Ivanoff recalled, would later join a mission trip to Siberia organized by a Covenant member in Alaska.

Ivanoff recalled that the pilot project was a lesson in faith. Along with the classes, students were learning how to be flexible and how to adapt when their plans fell apart—and to see how God might work in unexpected ways.

"It was a real-time, Alaska version of the Apostle Paul's missionary journeys," Ivanoff said. "It was tough because you're living out of a suitcase for almost three months because you're out in rural Alaska, you're not in charge of everything."

The sight of student leaders traveling from village to village and growing in their faith was encouraging for older Alaskan Covenanters to see, said Ivanoff. He said, that at times, local churches or other residents stepped up to help the students on their journey. At the end of the journey, Wilson and other church leaders organized a celebration for the students at First Covenant Church in Anchorage, to acknowledge the success of the program.

"These are young people participating in what God is doing, and growing in their faith while doing it, growing in knowledge," Ivanoff said. "They were learning but they were also experiencing what it means to lead, serve, and live within a Christian community."

That idea of Christian community was key for Paul Wilson for the Covenant's work in Alaska at a time when ACC went from a dream to a reality. In an interview with ACC's archivist, Wilson said the idea for Alaska Christian College was rooted in the church's long history of investing in young people—and his convictions about the power of the Christian community.

During that interview, Wilson said ACC drew inspiration from the legacy of Covenant High, as well as the work of Covenant missionary Ludvig Evald "L.E" Ost, who did leadership training in Alaska in the 1950s and 1960s. Inspiration also came from Rev. Don Erickson, Pastor of the Unalakleet Evangelical Covenant Church, who helped start Covenant Bible Camp, a long-running summer youth program in Alaska, in the 1960s.

"Investing in youth had been a big part of Covenant Church ministry, generationally," he said. "The Bible camp, CYAK, Alaska Christian College—are all of the same things."

The work of CYAK, Wilson said, was a precursor to the founding of ACC—because the ministry cared for students while creating a network of new leaders. Several of the staff who became part of the school's founding got their initial exposure to ministry from working with CYAK.

That idea of friendship among leaders tied into another core value that Wilson had—a belief in the power of what is called "compelling Christian communities." That kind of community, he told the ACC archivist in an interview, is built by Christians who believe in one another, who trust in Jesus, and hold the Bible at the center of life. And it's deeply relational with meaningful interaction between people of different ages, he said.

"Christian community in the best sense of the word—being the body of Christ," he said.

Wilson's view of the Christian community was shaped by the writings of Dietrich Bonhoeffer, the German theologian known for the book *The Cost of Discipleship*, as well as his opposition to Hitler. Bonhoeffer also ran a small seminary in the town of Finkenwalde in the 1930s. His experience there led to his book, *Life Together*. In that book, says Wilson, Bonhoeffer deals with the reality of "disillusionment" among Christians—the complicated work of building relationships with real people, who often don't live up to the expectations of those around him.

"It's one thing to dream of a beautiful community," said Wilson, "but another thing to build it. But no community can last without dealing with human imperfection," he said.

"Every human individual dream that is injected into the Christian community is a hindrance to genuine community and must be banished if genuine community is to survive," Bonhoeffer wrote in *Life Together*. "He who loves his dream of a community more than the Christian community itself becomes a destroyer of the latter, even though his intentions may be ever so honest and earnest and sacrificial."

"Instead of dreams of visionaries, the Christian community is built on a relationship with Jesus and gratitude for God's love," Bonhoeffer added.

"Because God has already laid the only foundation of our fellowship because God has bound us together in one body with other Christians in Jesus Christ, long before we entered into common life with them, we enter into that common life not as demanders but as thankful recipients," he wrote.

Along with helping young Alaskan Covenanters from Native communities grow in their faith, that kind of deep, intentional Christian community might be effective in addressing an ongoing concern that worried Wilson and other Covenant leaders. Few young people were going to college—and few of the students who went to college were succeeding. While not every young person needs to go to college, the percentage was so low that it was clear something was not working.

They hoped, in creating a Christian college in Alaska, to help students grow in their academic skills so that if they wanted to go on to further their college experience, they'd be better prepared to succeed—as well as helping them mature and grow in their faith.

"The hope was for Alaska Christian College to be a place where young people who are at that place of setting their course, their life course, would have a transformational experience of compelling Christian community," Wilson said. "The truth is, I think you get people together around the gospel and then you get good people to lead it. That is a predictor of a ministry's success."

For Alaska Christian College to become a reality, Wilson and other leaders of CYAK needed a plan and some evidence that the plan might succeed—which was one reason the pilot program was such a crucial first step. But they'd also need money and other resources to launch the school.

Wilson was thinking about this problem of funding during a trip to Chicago, where he was taking a retreat and doing some planning for the future. While there, he began working on a 5 to 8-page paper that would sketch out the case for what eventually became Alaska Christian College. With that document in hand, Wilson said he changed his travel plans. Instead of heading home to Alaska, he made a stop in Vancouver, Washington, a few hours out of Seattle, where he paid a visit to the M.J. Murdock Charitable Trust, a foundation with a long history of supporting nonprofits in the Pacific Northwest, including Alaska.

That paper detailed some of the Covenant's history of working with young people, including the impact of CYAK and work the church had done with students at the University of Alaska at Fairbanks, as well as the vision for the school, including profiles of possible staff.

"Leadership dynamics predict outcomes," Wilson liked to say. And he knew that if he got the right people, the school would have a chance to get off the ground.

At the top of the list for Wilson was Keith Hamilton, who he knew had the tenacity and the faith needed to tackle the job, followed by three young youth pastors who had become important leaders in CYAK: Curtis Ivanoff, Jeff Siemers, and Mark Hill.

With those four people on staff, the college might have a chance to get off the ground. And having them might convince Murdock to fund the project. Without naming them, he described the kinds of leaders the college would need in his proposal to Murdock—knowing that he had people in mind to fit the bill. He hoped the combination of data from the pilot project and the quality of the staff would convince Murdock to fund the school's start-up.

Getting Hamilton on board was key, in Wilson's eyes.

"I'd known Keith for a long time," Wilson said in his interview with ACC's archivist. "Keith was tenacious on mission. I really believed in him."

Along with his faith in nurturing a Christian community, Wilson also believed ambition played a role in getting any ministry off the ground. Not personal ambition, which Wilson believed was deadly for missions and ministry. Instead, ambition for a ministry's goals, he said, could help fuel success.

"Personal ambition is death to the soul and integrity and leads to pretense and arrogance and sometimes self-hate," he said in an interview. "However, ambition for the mission would keep the dream of the school alive in hard times and drive the school's staff to find solutions to even the most difficult challenges."

Hamilton also knew how to make friends and raise money—useful skills for a start-up college with big dreams but no donor base and few resources. He was tenacious, connected, and committed, Wilson said—three key traits Wilson felt would help Hamilton succeed.

2

With the pilot project completed and the proposal to Murdock Trust submitted, Wilson and other CYAK leaders turned their attention to finding a leader for the new college. Wilson was convinced early on that Keith Hamilton was the right person for the job, as did Bruckner, given their long relationship and Hamilton's past support for the work of CYAK.

But getting Hamilton on board took time. If the school was going to be a success, everyone needed to agree, including the Hamiltons. And that meant spending time together to see if the two groups were compatible and if Keith Hamilton's aspirations for what ACC could become matched with what leaders in Alaska wanted.

One of the first steps came in early June of 2000, when Hamilton was invited to serve as the guest speaker during the high school week at Covenant Bible Camp in Unalakleet. While there, he'd have time to get to know members of the task force working on the formation of Alaska Christian College. Once camp was done, the task force would then meet with Hamilton to discuss the possibility of becoming the school's first president.

Leading up to the trip, the Hamiltons had been praying for God's direction about a possible move to Alaska and what that would entail. The decision would not be an easy one. Even though the Hamiltons felt a call to mission work, they also loved serving at Arvada Covenant, a strong and vital church where they were doing important work. Leaving would not be easy, especially with three very young children and a three-legged dog to consider in the decision.

The Hamiltons were also keenly aware of the difference between being open to the opportunity to start a new ministry—and that opportunity becoming a reality. That lesson was made clear during Keith's discussions with Covenant Bible College about that school's Quito campus. In late 1999, Hamilton learned that CBC leaders had chosen Todd Slechta, his roommate from seminary, to lead that campus.

"For Deb and me, we felt a little disappointed, but knew that the Lord was in charge and that we were to stay in Arvada," Hamilton would write in his journal.

With the door to Ecuador closed, Keith reached out to Bruckner, following up on their earlier conversation about a possible Christian school similar to CBC in Alaska. During that time, Bruckner and other leaders were also working on a second project known as the Amundsen Education Center (AEC), named after a famed Covenant missionary pilot, Roald Amundsen, founder of the Missionary Aviation Repair Center (MARC) in Soldotna. That project would combine vocational training in carpentry and house building with the kind of Christian community offered by CBC.

In his journals, Hamilton recalled meeting with Steve Peterson, a longtime Covenanter and school teacher in Anchorage, while attending the Covenant's annual Midwinter Conference for pastors. That meeting regarding AEC went well, Hamilton wrote, but he had questions—in part because, though it had ties to the Covenant church, AEC was an independent nonprofit. That school was also set to open in Soldotna and Hamilton was skeptical about that setting, in that there were not Covenant churches in that area.

Later during that Midwinter meeting, Hamilton also had dinner with Paul Wilson, Curtis Ivanoff, and Neil Josephson, who was then the president of Covenant Bible College, to talk about possibilities for the future, especially about the possibilities for Alaska Leadership College—or ALC—as the school which became Alaska Christian College was then being referred to as.

That dinner went well, with Hamilton feeling a sense of connection with both the Covenant leaders from Alaska and their dreams for the school. "It seemed as if the Holy Spirit dropped right on us as we discussed and prayed about the ALC vision," Hamilton would later write.

Still, it was clear there was work that needed to be done. Josephson, Hamilton recalled in this journal, was supportive but felt that the school should be modeled closely after CBC. Ivanoff stressed the need for the school to reach Native students in Alaska, rather than Christian students in general. The relationship between the Covenant and the two potential schools—Alaska Leadership College and Amundsen Educational Center, and where Hamilton might fit in.

Not long afterward, things became clearer, as the board of AEC decided to move in a different direction away from Hamilton. However, Paul Wilson told Hamilton on the phone that the task force working on ALC was very interested in continuing their conversation with him.

"The door was now open for one option and closed on the other," Hamilton wrote in his journal. "Deb and I discussed what this could mean for us. I felt a tug but kept in my heart all that God was beginning to do in me. Our ministry at Arvada Covenant was going great, why would I even consider leaving? The most secure place to be in the world is in the center of God's will. I wanted to be in the very center of God's will."

The week at the Unalakleet Bible camp went well, with Hamilton feeling at ease among the students and youth leaders at the camp. One day, he and Marcus Reese, one of the youth pastors in Hooper Bay, went out for a hike with students to look for musk ox, a buffalo-like mammal that lives in the Arctic. The two had been talking about the possibility of a new college in Alaska and what it might mean for students. The topic had come up the day before at a meal, and that evening Hamilton said that Reese had dreamt that he and Keith were in McDonalds in Anchorage, and the conversation was that Keith would be coming to Alaska to lead the school. Wow, that had never happened to Hamilton before. A MIRACLE!

That same week, Hamilton went into town from camp and ran into Rick Hinkey, the pastor of the Unalakleet Covenant Church. Hinkey, who had run into Hamilton during past mission trips to Alaska, asked him when he might be moving to Alaska and that the Lord has spurred him to ask this question.

"Who told you to say this to me?" Hamilton would later recall asking. "Who is putting you up to this?"

"He said no one," Hamilton later wrote in his journal. "It was then I realized that God was using him to speak to me. I told Rick I was going to a task force committee meeting for the leadership of ALC. He was blown away, as was I." A MIRACLE!

Then, as Hamilton prayed, asking the Lord for one more sign, the unexpected happened. He and Debbie had been in Unalakleet at the end of Bible camp when he explained to Debbie all the miracles that were happening. They had dinner with Kathy Irvine, wife of MARC pilot Don, and their three children that last night in the village. Don was out flying so he didn't get to meet the Hamiltons. The unexpected happened a few weeks after the Hamiltons returned home from Alaska. Don Irvine's plane had gone down after dropping off a student (who later became an ACC student) and Jeff Siemers (ACC's current Executive Vice President), and Don passed in the solo crash. Upon hearing this news, both the Hamiltons' hearts were broken for Kathy and their kids, now friends. In fact, Kathy was pregnant with their fourth child and didn't know it when the Lord took Don home. The Hamiltons mourned this death along with all the Alaska faith family and the Hamiltons knew then and there that their hearts were with those who were mourning in Alaska. They sensed God used this tragedy to seal their hearts for Alaska.

A few days after the camp was over, Hamilton met with Wilson, John Hege, and Steve Peterson for an interview at the Evangelical Covenant Church of Alaska's (ECCAK) offices in Anchorage. The interview went well and eventually, Wilson and Hamilton set up plans for a second interview, this time with the General Council of the Covenant field in Alaska for later that summer. They also arranged for Hamilton to meet with about 80 Alaskan youth and leaders during CHIC, a national youth meeting for the Covenant, held once every three years in Tennessee. Hamilton again saw many of the same youth and continued to sense God pulling him toward working with this amazing group of students from mainly rural Alaska.

While waiting for that final interview, set for the end of August 2000, Hamilton began to speak with friends and denominational peers for advice and counsel, including Rev. Glenn Palmberg, then-president of the Evangelical Covenant Church denomination in Chicago. He also spoke with Neil Josephson, the president of CBC, asking for his counsel and help if Hamilton were to take on this new role—and receive his support. Finally, he also spoke with his old boss, Rev. Gary Walter, then-Executive Minister of Church Growth and Evangelism and later to become the denomination's president, for any support and assistance. Gary not only brought the case for opening the college to the front of denominational leadership, but he also presented a check to Hamilton at the Conference annual meeting in Eagle River in March of 2001. The gift from the denomination was $10,000! While there was doubt the college should open back in Chicago, where the Covenant denomination offices are based, Alaska Covenanters believed the time was ripe to start this adventure and ministry. A MIRACLE!

"This incredible gift to us was what I had prayed for and wished for," Hamilton later wrote in his journal. "CBC would assist us in all phases of our ministry and support our decisions as Neil would walk beside us all the way."

Not long before their final interview, Wilson telephoned with some bad news. While he and other leaders were eager to get the new college off the ground, the financial resources needed to make that happen were not in place. Because of that, he could not offer in good faith to call Hamilton into this new role—putting the start of the college into limbo. The call would be to serve as the President of Nothing—No students, funds, staff, or facilities.

After discussing and praying about the situation, the Hamiltons offered a potential solution. They were willing to raise one-half of the funds needed to support a move to Alaska and this new ministry.

"Paul agreed that this would be possible, but only if we remained in Arvada until June 2001," Hamilton wrote in his journal. "The risk would be lessened if we stayed in Colorado, raised support, didn't sell our home, and moved after we knew for sure the school would open in the fall of 2001."

With that option in place, Keith Hamilton made plans to travel to Alaska at the end of August 2001 to interview to become the President of Nothing.

The couple also began work on raising support, with an initial goal of having $28,000 in start-up costs in place. The first gift came out of the blue when Hamilton got a call from a longtime friend, Mike Tamte, who asked how things stood with the college. When Hamilton mentioned the need to raise support, his friend offered to send $1,000 to help out. It was a sign of things to come, Hamilton would later write in his journal.

This first gift was followed by a $3,000 gift from Tyler, a graduating youth from Hamilton's youth group in Arvada, followed by a gift of $10,000 from a church member mentoring Keith, and then another $5,000 from the mother-in-law of that mentor. By the time he left for the interview in Alaska, about half of the support needed was in place! Hamilton hadn't asked a single one of them for a gift. God provided. A MIRACLE!

After arriving in Anchorage, Hamilton spent the day with Trevor Simpson, a friend who had served as an intern for him in Arvada before moving to Alaska and was youth pastor at Mat-Su Covenant Church, Wasilla, Alaska. The two talked about the possibilities of Hamilton leading the college, with Simpson offering to serve on the school's board if Hamilton were to be called as president. The day ended with prayer, as Wilson and other Alaskan leaders prayed for Hamilton and the next day's interview.

"The morning came early and the sun was out bright and strong," Hamilton recounted in his journals. "I spent three and a half hours in an interview with the board. I was honest and answered questions with integrity. It was hard to read their faces, but I felt that they were affirming this project and its potential leader."

After taking a lunch break and an hour for deliberations, the board extended a call to Hamilton to be the first leader of the new college. At that moment, Hamilton knew he was being called to serve the church in Alaska, and knew the task ahead would be daunting. He was aware from the beginning that the school was not his project—but instead, a project and dream that belonged to the church in Alaska.

"Many people think it was my vision to plant ACC," he said in a 2011 interview with Seattle Pacific University, his alma mater, after receiving their Medallion Alumni Award. "Actually, it was the Native leaders and others of the Evangelical Covenant Church in Alaska who had the vision to reach this amazing group of young people forgotten by most of society. We were simply called to implement their vision."

Hamilton also felt a real sense of call to the school—and the challenges the school faced. "Yet," said Hamilton, "I knew that Deb and I were possibly the ones God wanted to move to Alaska."

Still, Hamilton returned home with a decision to make. On the flight home to Colorado following the interview, he brought with him a letter offering the job to lead a brand-new college. Now he and Deb had to decide whether or not to say yes. The board of ECCAK gave him a week to pray over the offer and then get back to them with a decision.

"A decision could not be my will, but only God's will," Hamilton later wrote, knowing that accepting the role came with a cost. "My deepest prayer was that God would now confirm the call in our lives to leave Arvada Covenant Church for mission service in Alaska. I loved my church and its youth and adults. It was family."

Hamilton flew back late on a Saturday night red-eye, arriving just in time to get to church the next morning in time for Sunday school, where the church's youth intern, Kory Moore, was teaching the 100 youth in the high school ministry. The message that Sunday was taken from the book of Judges, where Gideon is called to lead the Israelites in battle against the Midianites, who threatened to destroy them.

"I challenge each one of you, that if you are called by God to go to where He is sending you, you must go," Hamilton recalled Moore saying. That message was not meant for Hamilton, but he felt as if Moore were speaking directly to him.

A few days later, Hamilton met with Rev. Wes Swanson, the Pastor of Arvada Covenant Church, about the call to Alaska. Swanson, although saddened at the idea of Hamilton leaving, was supportive, especially after learning that the Hamiltons would likely stay in Colorado until the following summer. During that time, Hamilton would work part-time as interim youth pastor, giving the church time to find a replacement, while continuing to direct the youth intern program.

That led to a series of meetings with staff and youth group members, some of whom had traveled to Alaska on a mission trip and knew the importance of the work the Hamiltons would be doing. One student, Hamilton recalled, had recently inherited some money and decided to sign on to support the work of the new college in Alaska. Wow, another sign of God's provision!

After a trip to Grand Rapids, Michigan, for a wedding, the Hamiltons returned to Colorado, knowing that they were ready to say yes. That Sunday, Arvada Covenant happened to be holding a worship and prayer service—and afterward, Keith Hamilton went to the front altar to pray. While there, he was met by Harry Smith, the church chair, who had gotten wind that Hamilton might be leaving. After service, the two men talked into the night about the new college and what Hamilton would be doing. Hamilton left with Smith's blessing.

Two days later, he called Rev. Paul Wilson and accepted the call, only by the grace of God.

"It was simply easy, and refreshing, to have made the final decision," Hamilton recalled.

The next evening, Hamilton went to the church council meeting, where he announced his resignation and stepped into his new future. Not only did leaders at the church affirm the Hamiltons in their new role, but the church also decided to send them out as missionaries, pledging both support for their salaries and ongoing support for the college.

Not long after accepting the job, Hamilton made a decision that caused some headaches. He'd been tasked with coming up with an official name for the college and getting started on promoting the school. After talking with Paul Wilson and Trevor Simpson, Hamilton and they all settled on "Christian Bible College of Alaska" as the name for the school.

Because neither of them had started a college before, Wilson and Hamilton had decided to consult with Neil Josephson at CBC before making any major decision. The idea was to defer to Josephson's experience, especially in the college's early days—until they had a better idea of what they were going to be up against. Hamilton emailed the new name to Josephson, then followed up with a phone call to Quito, where the CBC president was attending the opening of their new campus.

When Josephson gave a verbal okay, Hamilton sprang into action. He sent out an email to friends and other colleagues, telling them about his new call and giving some details about the plans for the new college in Alaska. In that email, he mentioned that the new school would be loosely affiliated with Covenant Bible College—something he and Josephson had discussed but not finalized.

Before long, he began getting emails from folks at Covenant Bible College, wondering what exactly was going on. Other supporters looked at the initials for "Christian Bible College"—or CBC for short—and assumed wrongly that the new college was a campus of the Canadian-based college, which was not the case.

After conferring with Josephson, Hamilton realized that Christian Bible College was not going to work—and that a new email was needed, retracting the name, and apologizing for the confusion. Adding insult to injury, in his enthusiasm, Hamilton had also ordered $500 in t-shirts for the new college—which were now useless. He ended up donating them to families in Mexico on a future mission trip.

For a college with little money and few resources, it was a costly mistake.

While they appreciated the help of Josephson, the incident was a reminder that leaders of the new college had to distinguish between what they were doing and what Covenant Bible College was doing.

Wilson recalled having a difficult conversation about the college naming incident with Hamilton. However, rather than making him question the decision to hire Hamilton, Wilson said that the incident confirmed his faith in the college's new President.

"The trust of a leader comes from how they handle mistakes. And Hamilton handled this incident with grace and humility," Wilson told ACC's archivist.

"I had to talk with him," said Wilson, "and he was very apologetic. I think, if you asked him, it was a great learning experience. I just love how he handled it—he owned the whole thing."

That incident helped confirm that Hamilton had the right character for the job. He was entrepreneurial and a go-getter but was willing to listen and had the people skills needed to mend fences when needed. It also set the tone for the relationship between the two leaders—they could disagree and work things out.

"I would have had a hard talk with him, then go out the room and just start laughing," said Wilson. "And that's exactly why I like this guy."

There was some fallout from the incident. The board of CBC eventually decided against having an official tie between the two colleges. It was disappointing, but likely for the best, as both schools would face challenges in the years to come and their leaders would have their hands full. With great sadness to the ECC denomination and especially the Canada Conference of the ECC, CBC closed their doors a few years later due to financial issues. Praise God for the decades of faithful ministry of CBC that produced disciples, pastors, youth pastors, and missionaries.

Still, the two leaders, Josephson and Hamilton, remained close, something that Hamilton cherishes to this day.

"He has committed to me personally his support, wisdom, and friendship as he has in years past," Hamilton wrote in his journal. "He will be invaluable at that level, for sure, and for that I am grateful."

Hamilton also realized that he needed more enormous help in this new role. He was being asked to put together a college from the ground up, with few resources, with the need to be innovative and bold. Yet, he also needed Godly wisdom. For the first time in his life, he did not have a boss, at least on a day-to-day basis. He reported to the General Council of the Alaska Covenant Church and to Wilson—but they were not involved in the regular management of the college. That led him to seek out friends and other wise advisors, who could help avoid any unforced errors.

He described his dilemma this way, in a journal entry from the fall of 2000.

> "My prayer is that I will be wiser in my decisions, count the cost of some decisions, and seek wisdom from others," he wrote. "I am finding it hard to be the President of Nothing that doesn't exist, without a permanent name, and no funding. I also realize that the buck stops with me and I am used to having someone over me make the decisions. It is up to me and God's wisdom now. No one is really looking over my shoulder but the Lord."

Hamilton was also sent back to the drawing board in hopes of finding a new name for the college, which included asking for suggestions. One of the first hilarious suggestions was the "Alaska School of Scripture" that sounded great but had an unfortunate acronym and wouldn't look good on sweatshirts, which landed the name on the cutting room floor.

Wilson and Hamilton eventually settled on "Alaska Christian College" which seemed to fit—and eventually ordered new swag—t-shirts and sweatshirts—to help market the school. If one was to Google any Christian colleges in Alaska, guess what would always pop up at the number one spot! It was important that the name was not Alaska Covenant College as that would diminish its outreach across Alaska with "Christian" being much more inclusive. He needed to share the story of what God was up to at ACC. News of the school also began to leak out, with the Covenant's denominational news service publishing a brief article on plans for the college.

The name became official that fall when staff at the ECCAK offices filed paperwork to officially change the name of Alaska Leadership College to Alaska Christian College.

In the coming month, Hamilton would hit the road, visiting old seminary friends who were now pastoring churches in Kansas City, Minneapolis, Sacramento, and Bellevue, Washington, to raise support and share the story of what God was doing in Alaska.

He'd also start the crucial job of filling out the start-up staff for the college.

The most likely candidates were youth pastors already serving in Alaska—who already knew the ministry landscape and most importantly, were well known among students, a factor in developing that kind of trust needed for students to choose a start-up school. Bruckner recalled that Hamilton had the green light to recruit from CYAK staff and said that he encouraged leaders like Ivanoff, Hill, and Siemers to consider joining the staff at the college, knowing that the college needed all the support it could get.

One of Hamilton's first emails was to Mark Hill, who was then serving as a youth pastor in Nome. He hoped to convince Hill to join the college staff, to work on recruiting students for the new school. The fact that he was already based in Alaska was a big plus, given that Hamilton would be working remotely in Arvada until the following year.

Hill was open to the job but was concerned about the need to raise support, Hamilton recalled in his journals. He also had a line on a possible job in Minnesota and wanted to see how that turned out before further pursuing a role at the college. When that job fell through, Hill accepted a call as the school's first Director of Enrollment and Ministry Projects. In that new role, Hill would travel the state recruiting as well as planning mission trips for future students. He also hoped to do some career counseling for students once they finished at ACC.

Before that, Hill got to work raising the support needed for this new role and soon began as ACC's second employee, beginning December 1, 2000.

"Due to our lack of funds, we all have to raise support at this time and maybe into the future," Hamilton wrote in the fall of 2000, that single sentence summing up the tenuous nature of college finance in the early years. He and other leaders were aware that starting the college was a leap of faith and nothing was guaranteed.

Adding to the challenge was that none of the early staffers had ever worked in higher education. None were professors or administrators. Instead, they were a mix of ambitious and dedicated youth pastors and educators who wanted to create a community where young people could grow in their faith and gain the skills needed to shape their futures.

"It's the kind of thing where, if you wait until you are ready—you'll never be ready," Curtis Ivanoff said in a fall 2024 interview reflecting on his time at the college.

Still, even at the beginning, there were signs of hope. Cyndee Larson, a member of Arvada Covenant, signed up to be Hamilton's office assistant, becoming one of the school's first volunteers. Almost immediately she began work on getting business cards, letterhead, and a mailing list of supporters.

Slowly but surely, donations began rolling in, even before Hamilton's official start day of October 31, 2000.

"Today, I received a gift of $5,000 from a church family that had committed to do so. I feel so blessed and see God's hand upon us in every way," he wrote in his journal in mid-October.

By December, Curtis Ivanoff had signed on in a half-faculty, half-administrative role. Ivanoff recalled being surprised that he ended up joining the college start-up team. It was not exactly what he had planned. After graduating with a math degree from the University of Oklahoma, Ivanoff returned to his home state to take classes at the University of Alaska, so that he could be certified as a public school teacher, then returned home to Unalakleet to teach and, later, to be a pastor.

"I wanted nothing more when I was a young adult than to go back home," he said. By the time Alaska Christian College was being organized, that dream had come true. Ivanoff had taught in public school for three years, helped out with the youth at his home church, and then accepted a calling to pastoral ministry.

He had no plans to leave.

Still, Ivanoff was concerned about the health of the church statewide and particularly in youth ministry—and had been involved in CYAK for years. At the time when the discussions about ACC were taking place, Ivanoff was filling in as one of the leaders of CYAK, where Bruckner was taking some time off. Along with those two roles, he'd been part of what was essentially a task force working on getting ACC off the ground—searching for the school's first president, looking for a site that could house the school, and brainstorming about what the community and the culture of the school would be like. But that was as a supporter and planner, not someone who would be charged with helping bring the school to life.

"I wasn't thinking that I'd be involved directly," Ivanoff recalled.

Once Hamilton was hired and started officially on November 1, 2000, members of the task force kept meeting with him as the start-up plans took shape, said Ivanoff. During one of the meetings, in December of 2000, Keith described some of his vision for the school and invited Ivanoff to think about joining the staff.

"Keith, he can do these Jedi mind tricks," said Ivanoff years later, laughing about the experience and referring to a famed scene from the Star Wars movies.

All kidding aside, Ivanoff said one reason Hamilton had been chosen to lead ACC was his ability to invite other people to dream big for God and to see what God might do through their work. The school was not Hamilton's dream, though he played a crucial role as leader. Instead, from the beginning, he invited others to be part of making the school a reality—knowing that the work would be hard but was worth doing.

"One of Keith's gifts is drawing people into what God is doing," said Ivanoff.

After the conversation with Hamilton, Ivanoff said he called his wife, Kristi, to tell her about it.

"I told Kristi, 'I think I'm interested,'" Ivanoff said. "She was shocked."

A few months later, Ivanoff indicated that he and Kristi would accept a call to ACC.

"I was drawn to the vision," he said, "I had and still have a heart for discipleship, especially for young people."

He also knew that starting ACC was a job worth doing, even if all the plans were not yet in place.

That approach to ministry was not uncommon among Covenant Churches in Alaska. Leaders at CYAK had taken that same approach when they launched Alaska Leadership College as a pilot program. And in the 1950s, Ivanoff said Rev. Maynard D. Londborg, a Covenant missionary in Unalakleet, had started Covenant High because the community asked him to, rather than working through denominational channels, said Ivanoff.

While working on a history of the Covenant as a seminary student, Ivanoff had come to a letter written by leaders of the Covenant's World Mission department to Londborg in the 1950s, about what they called the "clandestine beginnings" of Covenant High School. Londborg had sent a copy of the school's inaugural yearbook to the head Covenant office in Chicago. Leaders there wrote back to express their surprise that the Covenant had a school in Unalakleet and wondered exactly what he was up to.

In a 2004 interview with Terrance Cole, a historian at the University of Alaska, Fairbanks, Londborg described the early days of Covenant High in the 1950s. When he arrived in Unalakleet as a missionary, there was no high school in the village, Londborg recalled. Instead, students who wanted to continue their education often went to boarding schools like Mount Edgecumbe High School in Sitka, more than 900 miles away.

Parents in the village remembered that missionaries had once run a grade school—and wondered if there was a way to keep their kids closer to home, Londborg recalled.

"They asked, 'Would you consider starting a high school?'" he said.

At first, Londborg thought about setting up correspondence classes for the students, through a program at the University of Nebraska. He wrote to the woman who was the head of Alaska's Department of Education for permission. She had a different idea.

"She fired a word right back, 'Well, if you're going to do that, why don't you order textbooks from our adopted textbook list and just start a high school and we'll put you on the approved list?'" he recalled. After some back and forth, mainly about making sure the school had the right credentials, Covenant High opened even before having certified teachers on staff.

That same entrepreneurial spirit was part of ACC's start-up culture. "Sometimes up here, you just have to move forward," Ivanoff said.

Earlier that fall, Hamilton had also reached out to Jeff Siemers, a former graphic artist who was serving as a youth pastor in Hooper Bay, Alaska, with a request. The college needed a logo; would Siemers consider working on it?

Siemers had played a key role in the "Alaska Leadership College" pilot project, traveling from village to village with a small group of students, and seemed a perfect fit to join the staff.

His time at Hooper Bay was also going to end the following summer—and Siemers had just begun thinking about what might come next. Whatever it was, Siemers believed he'd be staying in Alaska for the long haul. He'd moved up to Alaska a year earlier with Marcus Reese, who had come the previous summer to work at a cannery and to volunteer at Covenant Bible Camp—on what the two friends would refer to as his post-college "walkabout."

Reese was a teacher and had the summers off and had decided to do some traveling. He ended up at the Bible camp for a few weeks and got hooked on it. During his time at Bible camp, Reese had talked with Byron Bruckner and Paul Wilson about moving to Alaska and getting involved in ministry there. They gave him one piece of advice.

"They told him, if you're going to do something like this, you can't do it alone," Siemers said.

At the time, Siemers was working as a freelance graphic designer for some Chicagoland advertising agencies and was open to sharing an adventure with his friend. He had no debt and no major responsibilities to tie him down and decided to give it a go for six months.

In an interview in the spring of 2024, Siemers recalled that in February of 1999, just before they decided to leave, he'd gotten a job offer from a manager at one of the advertising agencies where he had been freelancing.

"I had to explain to him that I was moving to Alaska," he said.

Not long afterward, he and Reese piled their belongings into a Subaru and headed north, along with Reese's brother, Joshua, and his wife, who were going to work at First Covenant Church in Anchorage. The drive up was cold but beautiful, the weather clear with temperatures reaching thirty or forty degrees below zero at night.

With the help of engine block heaters and planning, and to make sure they stopped at hotels that were open during the winter, they made it to Alaska just in time to attend the ECCAK Annual Conference meeting in Scammon Bay before flying to Hooper Bay, where they arrived with little but the clothes on their backs. Most of their gear would be flown in later.

Before they left for Alaska, Paul Wilson had invited them to serve as youth pastors in Hooper Bay, a small village on the Bering Sea. From day one, they learned one of the first rules of life in rural Alaska—always be flexible. One reason why they'd been sent to Hooper was that there was no current pastor at the church, meaning the church parsonage was available for them to live in.

A few months after arriving, a new pastor was called to the church and needed the parsonage for his family. So the two youth pastors moved to a spare room at the church—and lived in that 10-by-15-foot space for the next 18 months.

"It was a storage room— the furnace storage room— and right in the back of the church," Siemers said.

During that time in Hooper Bay, the two youth pastors made friends in the community and hosted "Garlic Bread" nights on Saturday nights for the local youth group. They made pastoral visits, went hunting, and threw themselves into the life of the community. They also grieved alongside their new neighbors and saw first-hand the struggles that young people in the community faced—where many of the students in the church's young group had lost friends and family to suicide.

By 2001, with the new pastor settled into the community, Siemers and Reese felt their time in Hooper Bay had come to an end. About the same time, plans for the college were coming together. The pilot project had been a success and a grant application to M.J. Murdock Trust was still in the works.

While at Covenant Bible Camp that summer, Siemers began talking with Wilson and Hamilton about joining the staff—along with Mark Hill and Curtis Ivanoff. All three stayed at the school and helped lead the college through its start-up years. Mark and Joanna Hill stayed three years before leaving for North Park Theological Seminary, Curtis and Kristi Ivanoff stayed ten years before his call to be the Alaska Conference Superintendent, and Jeff Siemers is marking 25 years in July 2026.

While in Hooper Bay, Siemers said that he and Reese relied on lessons they learned from Bob McRae, who had been their youth leader at First Covenant Church in Rockford, Illinois, where the two grew up. Bob McRae would go on to teach youth ministry at Moody Bible Institute. Siemers said that McRae was the first person who'd ever asked him about going into Christian ministry.

Siemers recalled that one year, McRae had led a group from the church on a mission trip to Honduras to work with local churches. The plan had been for the team to split into three smaller groups, with each going off to stay with local families and work on a church project.

"There was a translation issue," Siemers recalled.

Instead of dividing into three groups—the team was split into groups of three. Siemers said that he and Reese, along with a friend, climbed in a truck and drove off to God knows where, leaving the youth group leaders wondering what had just happened.

"A local translator and a pastor and the three of us are just boom, gone," Siemers said.

The two friends had already done backpacking trips while growing up and saw the whole experience as an adventure. And they applied a simple, three-word lesson they'd learned as teenagers for how to get along in a new place: "Eat, drink, pray."

"That set the tone for us," Siemers said. "If someone sets something down in front of you, eat it."

Accepting the hospitality they found while in Honduras—and later in Hooper Bay—opened the door for relationships to begin. It also taught them how to adapt and survive.

That adaptability would serve Siemers—as did the independent and creative spirit that is common in Alaska—where people have a disdain for institutions while at the same time a dogged determination to build things on their terms.

"There's a great Oscar Wilde quote where he pities the person who becomes what they want to be because then their journey is finished," said Siemers. That kind of spirit, he said, was part of his own experience in building ACC. The school needed to exist, he said, and so the staff got to work on building it. They had what Wilson would call "an ambition for the mission."

3

With a leader in place, and the building blocks of the staff beginning to come together by late 2000, the search turned to finding a home for the college. This was a challenge, in large part because the school had few resources and needed a place large enough to house and feed a few dozen students as well as space for classrooms. For a temporary office, the upstairs "crow nest" at Community Covenant Church in Eagle River became the first "home" for the start-up of ACC. Rev. Mark Meredith, lead pastor, and Sandy Gold, church treasurer, invested time, space, and resources for ACC in its first fledgling months. That church has always been the number one supporter financially in the state for the mission of ACC and has been so for all of ACC's 25 years.

At first, Wilson and other leaders thought that the school could find space at a camp or lodge, which sent them to search across the state for spaces that might be underutilized and available.

One of the first places they visited was the facility owned by Interact Ministries in Palmer, Alaska, a beautiful location on Lazy Mountain, but too small for the college's needs. During the visit, Hamilton and other ACC leaders learned that it could house as many as 30 students, but only if they slept three to a room. The space was only going to be available for about a year, which could have bought the college time to find a permanent space.

In December, a group of about six of the ACC task force leaders traveled to the Kenai Peninsula, to look at property in a small community in Kasilof, about 15 minutes south of Soldotna. They'd reviewed a listing for the property online, sent to Hamilton by an Arvada friend, and on the surface, it seemed a good fit. It had 26 bedrooms, was across the street from a lake, and had an airstrip. What could be more Alaskan? So, on a cold and wet morning, Wilson and the other task force leaders, including the Hamiltons who had come all the way from Colorado, flew down from Anchorage to have a look because the roads driving down to the Peninsula had questionable conditions.

Things did not go well.

"It was just a mess," Wilson recalled years later. The space was large enough but had significant structural issues and proved a disappointment. Hamilton stated it looked like a junior higher had planned it as a part of their drafting class.

During the visit to the Kenai Airport, Debbie Hamilton picked up a copy of a real estate magazine that Paul Wilson handed her about homes for sale and came across a listing for a house at 35109 Royal Place in Soldotna. Since they were in town, the group decided to take a look. After a call to the realtor, they quickly arranged a tour before flying back to Anchorage, disappointed in what they had seen in Kasilof. Since the power was off at the house, the group did a walk-through by flashlight. While the property was impressive, so was the price tag—so high that most of the group was almost immediately turned off.

Not Hamilton and Wilson.

"They all said, 'No, no, no, no, no,'" Wilson recalled. "Keith and I looked at each other and said, 'This is it.' We just didn't say anything to anyone else."

The 8,400-square-foot house, on a large, 10.5-acre wooded estate, had five bedrooms, a spacious living room, and even a swimming pool with more space on the site to expand. Above the swimming pool was a plywood cover on steel cords that doubled as a putting green, which could be lowered down from the ceiling. The location was perfect—only a block from the local community college and not far from two nearby airports, making it accessible for students and staff, also with four mission agencies flying throughout Alaska. A local nonprofit, Central Peninsula

Counseling Services, owned the site and had invested several hundred thousand dollars to convert the property from a single-family home into a space that could legally house students overnight. Even better, there was plenty of room on the property to enlarge the college throughout its 10.5 acres.

"A huge cathedral ceiling is what you see first when you enter the home," Hamilton would write later in his journal. "I sensed immediately that this is the perfect facility for ACC to plant."

The property on Royal Place did present some challenges.

Wilson and other leaders had hoped to rent a space while the college got off the ground. But the owners wanted to sell, not rent. And there were no Covenant churches within several hours of the campus, meaning the school would be cut off from the broader Alaska Covenant community in its crucial start-up phase. There was also moisture damage to the siding of the building, which would need to be addressed.

Still, Hamilton and other leaders believed they had found the right spot. Their hopes for the space were strengthened after a second walk-through with Dave Peterson, a local Covenant contractor originally from Colorado, who had agreed to help them with the property search. Hamilton would later recall feeling a sense of peace about the future of the campus, as well as being cognizant that buying the property would come with a significant cost.

"We cannot be full of excitement and cash poor," he would later write in his journal.

The college, with the help of Rob Hall, an attorney working for National Covenant Properties, would eventually negotiate to purchase the property for $345,000, $45,000 below the initial asking price after Hamilton committed to raise the mortgage funds. That is $41 a square foot on 10.5 pristine wooded acres! A MIRACLE!

The purchase was made possible with the building's original owner, Leonard Ballard, agreeing to let the college take over the balance of a $345,000 mortgage at eight percent interest which was already in place. Leonard was a part of the Worldwide Church of God, some would consider a cult, but committed his life to Christ along with his fellow church members, getting baptized in his own pool.

Thus, the deal was set for the college to begin making payments of $2,800 a month, beginning in April 2001. But how was the $25,000 down payment going to be made? What miracle would God do to provide in this extraordinary need and vision?

Those first days after the agreement had been made, with no money to put down, Hamilton flew to First Covenant in Portland, Oregon, to preach and share the vision of ACC. He had no videos, photos, brochures, student testimonies, or a plan in how to secure the down payment. The Lord was way ahead of him again. After the morning message, the pastor, Rev. John Wenrich, took Hamilton out to lunch with the mission board of the church. When the time was right, Hamilton asked if the church would consider gifting up to $25,000 to buy ACC. They said they would get back to him. Ugh. That could mean a big no. Yet, God was way ahead of this plan and Hamilton received a call from Pastor Wenrich, who would later become the ECC's denominational president, who exclaimed, "The check's in the mail!" Hamilton inquired how that could be. Unbeknownst to him, the church had just sold its own little Bible camp, Molalla Retreat, and wanted to do some significant gifts with the sale's earnings. The church had a business meeting soon after Hamilton was there in Portland to decide on how to best bless other ministries and they decided to buy a college! A MIRACLE!

Hamilton, like any fundraising person, knows to thank those who give sacrificially to ministry, and this was no exception. A year after the first class graduated, he returned to First Covenant Portland to preach again and thank the congregation, this time with stories, a video, and photos of the college they bought. After the service, an elderly lady named Esther Hallock, came up to Hamilton to tell him "the rest of the story." She was the last living charter member of the church, in her 90s, and she was the one who stood up at the meeting to proclaim the funds must go to plant ACC. When asked why she stood, she explained to Hamilton that she may be the only person remaining alive that remembered that their church, at the turn of the 20th century, was planted by none other than the first Covenant missionary to Yakutat, Alaska! She said, that in his honor and memory, the church had no choice but to make the full down payment. A MIRACLE!

Another key step in the college's development was now complete.

"I am elated at the price, the location, and the Lord's goodness to ACC and the students of the Covenant Church and other churches of Alaska," Hamilton wrote in his journal. "Now I need to remember that 'unless the Lord builds the house, the builders labor in vain.'"

Much of Hamilton's first year on the job was spent on the road, raising funds and navigating the complicated world of denominational politics. He had been hired to lead the new college in part because of his deep network of contacts within the Evangelical Covenant denomination. Yet, many of the people he knew, especially in the Midwest Conference, where Arvada Covenant was located, were already supporting schools like North Park University or the new CBC campus in Windsor, Colorado, which Hamilton had helped start.

That meant he had to be careful in how he went about fundraising—as he did not want Alaska Christian College to be seen as a rival to those other schools, especially because those schools were also key partners. He and other ACC leaders knew they'd depend on the support and mentorship of Neil Josephson and other leaders at CBC as they got the Alaska college off the ground—and Hamilton hoped that some future ACC grads would possibly make their way to North Park University, as some had done, as NPU accepted 100 percent of ACC's classes toward their credits needed for graduation.

Along the way, there were small signs that momentum was building for the college. During a visit to Shawnee, Kansas, where his friend Rev. Kenton Johnson was a youth pastor, a church member offered to send $200 a month in support for the college, while others expressed interest in learning more about the school.

Other small gifts began to roll in. A staffer at Arvada Covenant pledged $2,000 in support, while another family from Colorado pledged $5,000. Another friend from Hamilton's time in seminary pledged $2,000. While Hamilton was visiting in San Diego at Covenant Village there, another $25,000 in pledges came in from a couple that loved Alaska. Wherever Hamilton went, there seemed to be interest in the college's success. Many would say how much the mission to Alaska meant to them and to their giving.

By the end of the year, about $65,000 had been raised for start-up costs, with another $40,000 hopefully on the way, while $33,000 was already out the door in getting the work off the ground—a reminder that the school had little margin to operate.

Much of the college's future, at least in the short term, depended on the outcome of a grant request for about half a million dollars, which Wilson had made to the Murdock Trust. Wilson had been keeping staff at the Trust updated on the progress at the school, including the plans to purchase the property on Royal Place, and felt good about the possibility that the grant would be approved. But an official vote by the Murdock Trust trustees would not come until the spring of 2001, if not later, meaning the start-up team was still working mostly on faith without dollars. Fortunately, one of the trustees, Lyn Swanson, was a member of the McMinnville Covenant Church in Oregon, and desired to put forth an effort to see if ACC could be funded.

Just after Thanksgiving of 2000, Hamilton made a trip to Covenant Bible College, Strathmore, Alberta, to get a closer look at running a college. There he spent several hours in a frank discussion with Josephson about some of the issues that college students were dealing with, including issues of mental health, and for which staff at ACC would need to be prepared and for which students would need support.

Hamilton also left CBC with copies of class syllabi, admission policies, and a host of other documents, all of which could be adapted for use at ACC. He also had the chance to meet with Alaskan students at the college, who were pleased to hear about the plans for the new school.

"I have seen and heard and learned many things these past three days," Hamilton would later write in his journal, reflecting on his time at CBC, "I almost believe I can, with the Lord's help, plant this college. Students will come. Faculty will want to serve. Donors will step forward."

Years later, Ivanoff remained grateful for CBC and the impact that school had on the early days of Alaska Christian College, especially with the Alaska school's focus on "whole-life discipleship." During his early days teaching at the school, he often relied on class notes and other materials that the CBC professor had shared with him and other teachers. That support from CBC gave Ivanoff and other staffers the reassurance that they were not on their own and didn't have to invent everything at the school from scratch.

"We wanted to be just like Covenant Bible College," he said. "From my perspective, we placed the Covenant Bible College program on the Xerox machine and pressed the green button."

During the start-up process, other key staffers kept coming on board. Eva Oyoumick, from Unalakleet, signed on to be the Dean of Women, with Jeff Siemers agreeing to be the Dean of Men, filling two key roles with direct contact with students. Curtis Ivanoff was on board along with Mark Hill, whose main role was recruiting students.

Hill also played a key role in bringing Alan and Sharon Finifrock, a pair of longtime Covenanters and public school educators in Alaska, to ACC. He had been out on a recruiting trip and had stopped over in the community of Toksook Bay, on Nelson Island, about 100 miles west of Bethel. He'd come in on a morning flight, with plans to give a presentation at the school where the Finifrocks worked, before traveling to Mekoryuk, a village on nearby Nunivak Island, where there was a Covenant Church.

But the weather turned, and Hill ended up stranded for about five days in Toksook Bay sleeping on the floor in the gym, and spent much of that time working on developing materials for the college. During that time, Alan Finifrock would bring him dinner in the evenings, and they'd end up talking late into the night.

"I asked him a lot of hard questions," Finifrock told the ACC archivist in an interview.

The mission of the college appealed to the Finifrocks, who were just about to retire from the public school system. The couple had first come to Alaska in the late 1960s to teach for a number of years and then had returned home to Duluth, Minnesota, where they had become involved with a Covenant church. In the 1990s, they returned to Alaska to teach, in part because they'd be eligible for pension and insurance if they did so.

Alan had landed a job as an administrator at the school in Toksook Bay, while Sharon got a job teaching English and Social Studies at the high school in the small Yup'ik speaking community. Taking that role had been a stretch for Sharon. She'd spent most of her career teaching in primary schools but in Toksook Bay, those grades were taught in Yup'ik, a Native language she did not speak.

She'd also been intimidated by the idea of working with high school students.

"Now I had said that I would never teach high school—I just didn't want anything to do with that," Sharon would recall in an interview with ACC's archivist. "But I felt confident that I could teach English, because that had been my second choice for a career."

Armed with textbooks and a willing attitude, Sharon Finifrock took on the role of a high school teacher and was surprised to find that she was thriving in it. The high school was small, with only about 30 students, and Finifrock found she was able to connect with students in that kind of smaller setting. Because of the smaller class sizes, she was able to get to know the students and some of the challenges they faced, and found she enjoyed being with them.

"I learned to love them and how to relate to them," she said.

Still, at times, she wondered what she—and God —were doing.

"It's way out on the southwest coast, and there's no trees there because there's too much wind all of the time," said Sharon. "And I remember walking home at night, overlooking the ocean, and praying, 'Lord, why in the world do you have me here teaching high school?'"

That time in Toksook Bay proved to be essential training for the Finifrocks, preparing them for their time at ACC, where they became seen as trusted elders and grandparent figures for some of the students and parents to the staff. During their time in Toksook Bay, the Finifrocks were reminded of the importance of trusting relationships in the lives of students. Even from the beginning, those relationships proved to be the crucial ingredient in shaping what Alaska Christian College would become.

"The staff invested in the lives of the students," she said.

The Finifrocks were also drawn to the school's focus on Alaska Native students, in part because of an experience they'd had early in Alaska. During the 1960s, they were teaching in the town of Glennallen, where a Christian group had started up a Bible college. While the school wanted to reach Native young people, that had proved a challenge—and so many of the students at the school came from the lower 48. While that helped with enrollment, students from Alaska felt overwhelmed in that setting—and the school lost its focus, said Alan Finifrock.

As retirees, the Finifrocks also had pension and insurance in place—making the idea of taking what was essentially full-time volunteer roles doable. When the weather finally cleared, Hill left Toksook Bay, with a pledge to connect the couple with Hamilton. After some emails and a dinner in Bethel with Hamilton, who flew in to meet them, they were ready to join up. By June of 2001, they'd mailed about 80 boxes of their belongings to Soldotna and made plans to move.

In July 2001, while spending time back in their home area in Minnesota, the Finifrocks stopped by their alma mater, the University of Northwestern. While Alan found his way to the Academic Vice President's office, Sharon found her way to the library and introduced herself to the Director of Library Services, Dale Solberg. Sharon began to tell who she was and that she and her husband were to be volunteer staff members at a new Bible college in Alaska. Dale knew exactly what she was talking about because of his long interest in Alaska mission and that, just a few days earlier, his church, Salem Covenant Church in New Brighton, Minnesota, had carried a newsletter article and ad calling for faculty, staff, volunteers, and financial support for Alaska Christian College. After an hour's visit with Sharon, the discussion resumed that evening for another three hours with both Alan and Sharon at a nearby restaurant, where they talked about the school's nascent library and many other aspects of Christian higher education. Solberg recalls, "The Holy Spirit was stirring in me, and it crossed my mind that someday I might be called to serve in Alaska." Solberg advised Sharon on implementation of library services at a Bible college in a follow up document in August 2001 and then continued email communication with Sharon for the next three years. He also began receiving the ACC monthly email updates and development letters, undertook several fundraisers to rebind and ship red and blue Covenant hymnals for the ACC chapel, and met with and urged the Mission Commission at Salem Covenant to begin supporting ACC.

Bringing the Finifrocks on board proved a game changer, Paul Wilson would later say. Unlike most of the other college staff—who'd mainly been youth workers—they brought a wealth of experience in education and Godly wisdom.

"We would have completely screwed up without Alan and Sharon," Wilson said. "Alan knew what he was doing. These are humble people, with more cultural sensitivity. Without Alan, the whole thing would have been a disaster."

When they arrived on campus, the college was very much a work in progress. For the first few weeks, the Finifrocks found themselves sleeping on the floor and working out of makeshift office spaces.

"My first desk was a four-drawer file cabinet in the laundry room," Alan Finifrock recalled. Alan was named Director of Operations and was charged with trying to bring some organizational structure to a start-up institution. Sharon was given a more pragmatic role, keeping everyone fed.

Sharon became the school's first Director of Food Services a bit by accident. In the early days of ACC, before the college opened for classes, the school was as much a camp as a college, she said, with everyone pitching in where they were needed, and often making do with few resources and a boatload of ingenuity.

"We were scrambling ahead of time to get everything ready and done," she told the ACC archivist in an interview.

At the time, Debbie Hamilton and Kristi Ivanoff, both of whom would be teaching and providing counseling to students, were putting together meals for the staff. But both had young kids, as did Joanna Hill, who was going to serve as the campus nurse as well as working as a nurse in the community. The one other staff member's wife was in her 70s, Phyllis Michelson, from Washington.

The plan, Finifrock learned, was to have the wives of the staff take turns making meals.

"I thought, that's not going to work," she recalled saying. "So I said to Keith, I'll do it."

Finifrock, who was then in her 60s, cooked for the first quarter of the school, as she didn't have any other obligations on campus that first quarter. Along with cooking, she ordered food and did all the meal planning, until the school could recruit a cook to take over later in the year. Ira Isaac came from Mekoryuk to fulfill that need after Sharon.

At that point, she moved to more of an administrative role, doing some office work and running the school's first library. Part of the role also included ordering textbooks for the students as well as finding a place in the crowded building for a library.

"We did not have a library, we did not have a room, we didn't have shelves, and we didn't have books," she said. "That's kind of the story of ACC—we just go ahead without any of this."

Finifrock and the library got a break during a visit to Kenai to pick up some greeting cards at a local pharmacy that was going out of business. The pharmacy area was filled with shelves.

"I think we could utilize those," she recalled thinking at the time. "We purchased those shelves for practically nothing and brought them over." A MIRACLE!

While she was negotiating for the shelves, Finifrock noticed the store had a refrigerated cooler used for storing soft drinks and asked if it too was for sale. It was, and so she picked it up as well, installing it in the college's kitchen, where it is still used to this day.

"We did a lot of that, just finding and scrounging what we could, and trying to figure out how this could be used and utilized until a later time," she said.

By the summer of 2001, the Hamiltons had finally sold their house in Arvada, packed up, bought a house in Soldotna, and started making their way to Alaska. They found a campus that was very slowly taking shape. Hamilton was the first to arrive, joining Mark Hill in a nearly empty building on campus during some of the longest days of the year in early June, with daylight lasting nearly around the clock. Hamilton's arrival date was June 10, 2001, flying in from Denver after preaching his last sermon and a farewell party.

"We (Mark Hill and I) were both sleeping in the walk-in closets in the building as there were no windows and it is very light outside!" Keith Hamilton wrote in his journal. "We now have a 8,400-square-foot mansion we are living in with a total of two chairs, one Costco table, two laptops, and one splitter line going into our cheap combo phone/fax/copier machine with a 4,800 bps dial-up."

By mid-summer, the first members of the staff were on campus. The rest of the Hamilton family arrived on June 20 and the whole family slept in sleeping bags on the floor of one of the bedrooms until they could move into their first Alaskan home. The Ivanoffs arrived from Unalakleet, and the Finifrocks were joined by retired volunteers Bob and Phyllis Mickelson, with Jeff Siemers and Eva Oyoumick filling out the staff. They all began their work on July 1, 2001, preceded by Mark Hill and Hamilton who began off-site in late 2000.

Student applications also began rolling in that summer—with 18 students having expressed interest by early June and school leaders were hopeful that twenty students in all might enroll that fall. Now they just had to get things ready for their arrival with an empty house void of furniture, books, kitchen supplies, beds, etc. By opening day, the house would be full of all those items it needed in order to open its doors. A MIRACLE!

For the first year, the plan was for all the students to sleep in the main house, with the boys all sharing the rec/pool room—with the pool covered and bunk beds lining the walls. The beds had been one of the unexpected blessings that showed up in the early days. While speaking at Harbor Covenant Church in Gig Harbor, Washington, Hamilton met up with a furniture salesman named Bill Lemke whose territory included Alaska. After hearing the school's story, Lemke decided he could lend a hand.

"He found a company in Soldotna, Sadlers, that will donate a partial container full of furniture to ACC and get all our beds for us at cost and shipped free!" Hamilton recalled in his journal. "Praise God!" A MIRACLE!

As summer rolled on, the campus began to take shape. Rod Butler, a volunteer from Rocklin Covenant Church, California, where Hamilton had begun a career as a youth pastor, and Gary and Susan Palmer, volunteers from Arvada, came up to Soldotna to help with putting together a campus plan, including setting up a kitchen and exploring options for student housing. Butler also installed the first satellite dish on the roof of the main building.

Part of that plan included building student and student life staff housing so that not everyone would be living in the same building after the first fall. After looking at options like yurts, tent-like structures that originally were developed in Central Asia, school leaders decided to build three cabins on the main grounds to house students and staff.

This began what would become a summer tradition at ACC—harnessing the power of summer church volunteer groups to build up the campus. The first to arrive in the summer of 2001 was a team from Community Covenant Church in Shawnee, Kansas, with plans to build three 18-by-24-foot cabins to house the male students. Along with the labor, Community Covenant raised $25,000 to pay for materials.

The weeks before the arrival of the first work team were a blur, with equipment rentals to prepare the foundations for the cabins, a rush to get approvals for the construction project in order, and a race to get the go-ahead from the State of Alaska to operate as a college.

"We are getting a lot done and nothing done," Hamilton would later recount in his journals.

Registering as a college with the State was a particular concern. To open in the fall, the college needed approval from the State of Alaska—something Paul Wilson admitted he neglected to do in the rush to get the college ready for opening. Wilson, in an interview with ACC's archivist, recalled showing up at the offices of the Alaska Commission on Postsecondary Education with his hat in his hand and asking for help.

"They let me sweat," Wilson recalled before the staff told him that they could help get the needed approvals.

Money was also a constant challenge that summer, with funds being spent almost as soon as they came in. By the time a second work group from Shawnee, Kansas, had framed in the first two cabins, more than half of the initial $25,000 for the project was gone—and the buildings did not have roofs—with both the Finifrocks and Jim Engwall, a volunteer supporter from California, out on the road raising funds for the school's library.

Another group from Castle Oaks Covenant, Castle Rock, Colorado, arrived in time to frame out the third cabin while leaders at ACC waited for the roof trusses to arrive. School leaders also worked on getting approval from the State Fire Marshal's office to renovate the school's kitchen—which had been delayed. That meant problems, as a team from Arvada Covenant was on its way to work on the project and had to be reassigned.

By mid-July some good news arrived. On Friday the 14th, the phone rang in Keith's office.

"Is this the president of ACC, the newest religious-exempt postsecondary educational institution in Alaska?" Paul Wilson, who was on the other end, asked. The college was approved as a religious-only institution, which meant, among other things, that a $2,500 fee was waived. A MIRACLE!

A pair of grants totaling $10,000 arrived in late July just in time to keep the construction project moving forward, followed by approval from the fire marshal for the kitchen renovations. Just when things seemed to be ready but then came to a grinding halt, the solution always seemed to show up just in time.

"This has, again, strengthened me greatly in my trust that God wants ACC to open up this fall with a full student enrollment," Hamilton wrote in his journal. "It is crazy how doubtful we become when we see walls before us. Our God pushed walls down to make way for His will."

Still, the combination of general contracting the cabins, overseeing the renovations, and working on the education program at the college took its toll on the staff. There was always too much to do and never enough time. Hamilton and other leaders were made constantly aware of how much they did not know. For example, the cabins were mostly completed when ACC leaders learned that they needed to also have the plans reviewed by the Alaska State Fire Marshal's office. Hamilton recalls speaking on the phone with the State Deputy Fire Marshal who was hearing saws in the background as the conversation continued. The deputy asked Hamilton what that noise was in the background, to which he quietly said, "Construction on the cabins." Oops. The deputy stated that ACC was to immediately stop the construction until the plans were approved by their office. Another mistake by ignorance.

Help arrived in the form of a volunteer named Bruce Schock, an architect from Arvada Covenant, who worked on the cabin and plans for the remodeling of the main house. One lesson Hamilton took away from the experience was the need to recruit more experienced help early on for major building projects, as he had neither the skill nor the time to oversee such projects, raise funds, and cover the school's programming.

The work moved on and by August, the cabins were closed in, dry walled, and insulated. Bob Bode, an 80-year-old volunteer from Arvada Covenant, who had overseen the church's work crew, offered to come back on and help get the job done. Once again, help showed up at the right time, as supporters continued to sign on to the college's mission.

Meanwhile, the staff had turned to getting the educational program at the college off the ground in the five weeks that remained before opening. That meant preparing syllabi, ordering books, and getting class lectures ready, which was a challenge since everyone would be teaching college students for the first time when classes started.

Five weeks before the opening, it was also unclear how many students would show up. Hamilton and other leaders prayed for an initial group of 20 students to be in place by September 17, the first day of class. However, the list of students was still not finalized.

Late August also brought the long-awaited news that the Murdock Trust had approved a $493,000, three-year grant for the college to fund staff and provide a stable base of funding in the college's early years. A MIRACLE!

The grant was based largely on the proposal that Wilson had first made when ACC was still a dream in the eyes of Alaskan leaders, and Murdock had provided coaching during the college's first year. Wilson, for example, had spoken with staff at the Trust when the college was considering buying the Royal Place property and gotten their approval for the purchase. So, Wilson and Hamilton had hopeful expectation that the grant would be approved.

Getting the news the grant was in place was a huge milestone and all but ensured that the college would open on time. The grant came with challenges, as the college was required to raise an additional amount in matching funds. The grant did not cover essentials like food, scholarships, books, and other needs—all of which weighed heavily on the minds of the staff, as did more immediate concerns like making payroll.

"We are desiring to do ministry whatever the cost—but I need wisdom as to how to raise these funds and make a difference in Alaska," Hamilton wrote in his journal. "It is God's vision and we pray continually for His provision."

On September 11, 2001, as the college staff prepared for opening day the following week and some board meetings scheduled around the dedication, the staff began to get word that something terrible had happened in New York City. Hijackers took control of four planes—crashing two into the World Trade Center towers, causing their collapse and the death of thousands. Another plane crashed into the Pentagon, while on the fourth plane, a hijacking and passenger revolt led to a crash in a Pennsylvania field.

Airline flights were canceled nationwide—leaving a number of students headed to ACC stranded, as well as board members and many of the denominational guests who planned to attend the school's dedication, set for Sunday, September 16.

"I walked into the office at ACC Tuesday morning (September 11) to see photos on the internet with the staff," Hamilton wrote, recalling the terrorist attacks and all that followed in his journal. "In horror and shock, I stood with our staff in solemn disbelief."

In the end, only five members of the school's new board could attend the dedication, which was barely a quorum. Still, Covenanters from Alaska rallied to support the college. The board meeting also brought a gift for the staff, who were granted extra vacation time and a pay raise to reward their hard work.

Then, Sunday the 16th arrived, with 85 people, including 15 of the initial class of 22 students, who gathered on campus that morning for worship in the living room (named the Denali Room) of the main house on campus, with Paul Wilson preaching. Worship was followed by lunch and tours and surprise afternoon rain showers—which caused a last-minute move of the outdoor dedication service to nearby Peninsula Grace Brethren Church.

"We 'bugged out,' grabbing everything, and headed over to Peninsula Grace Brethren Church where all 200 plus people met us for an hour and a half of song, testimony, worship, dedication, special music, and offering," Hamilton later recalled. "What a moment together." Ben Schoffmann, who led the worship service that memorable day, would later become an important part of the college's future as the vice chair of the President's Advisory Council.

4

The first week of classes at Alaska Christian College began with a day of rest—in part to give the staff a moment to catch their breath after the rush to get the campus ready to open, and in part to give those whose travel was delayed by the 9/11 terrorist attacks one more day to get to campus. Now the real work of the college began, and with the beginning of classes came a growing realization of the challenges that lay ahead.

After a week of getting to know the students with chapel services, orientation sessions, dinners, small groups at staff homes, and Friday night s'mores on the Kenai beach, the students settled in for classes and felt for the first time the pressure of being in classes.

Things did not go well, with most of the class failing a simple quiz in a class on discipleship taught by Hamilton, with most of the students admitting they had not studied, even though they'd been warned about the quiz. The good news was that, given a second chance to study, most of the students aced the quiz.

Hamilton and other leaders had known that many of the students who would attend ACC might struggle and need help in shoring up their study habits and time management as well as some of their academic skills. The experience was a reminder of why the college was needed as well as a real-time example of the kinds of support students would need.

Behind the scenes, the school's financial pressures remained a constant reality. Though the Murdock grant had been approved, the funds took time to arrive, putting the school in a cash flow crunch. Along with teaching, Hamilton was still out raising funds, with $25,000 needed to pay off the cabins and more funding needed for ongoing expenses. By November, Hamilton had been out on the road for nearly six weeks raising funds by speaking in churches—and eventually the Lord provided a total of $35,000; $10,000 over the goal for the cabin project.

Meanwhile, the college staff was busy teaching and dealing with some of the common issues of college students away from home for the first time, like underage drinking and homesickness, as well as providing support and counseling for students.

School leaders found themselves trying to balance their hopes to disciple students and help them grow in their faith by creating a supporting and loving community that helped students grow rather than removing those who struggled. By Christmas, three of the original 22 students had left campus and the staff was uncertain about how many students would return after the new year for the last two quarters remaining.

And there were bills to pay—the school would end the calendar year with $3,000 in unpaid bills—and the need to raise about $20,000 to get through January.

Finding the right identity became a constant challenge in the early days of ACC, said longtime staffer Jeff Siemers, who began as dean of men and eventually became the executive vice president and one of the few staffers to remain at ACC throughout its first two decades. He said that in the school's first few years, faculty had to balance the school's two main goals: creating a supportive Christian community that fostered spiritual formation and discipleship, and providing an academic environment that prepared students for future education and work.

The faculty and staff were also leading small groups of students in their homes every week—meaning that they had to balance the roles of being professors, small group leaders, and college administrators all at the same time.

During those early years, staff like Siemers were also forging an identity for the school in real time. He said they often had to ask themselves, what exactly were they building? Was it a college, a spiritual community, a camp, or a developmental program for students, with intensive counseling and academic support services?

That question often came up with discussing cases of student discipline. Students at ACC—like students at every college, Christian or otherwise—sometimes ran afoul of the rules, especially rules around issues like the use of alcohol. They, like their peers at other schools, often came to school with hurts from the past or mental health concerns. The school was started at what has become a major mental health crisis among college students in the United States—though the staff at ACC did not know it at the time. President Hamilton stated that he had seen more issues of discipline, pain, and struggles in the first quarter of ACC than he had seen cumulatively from his first 20 years in youth ministry.

Siemers recalled that cases of student discipline often were complicated— with staff trying to figure out what would be best for the students' welfare and development as well as the well-being of the entire community.

The first few months at ACC also required a lot of flexibility and ingenuity. In the early days, all of the 22 students in that initial class lived in what had once been a single-family home at 35109 Royal Place in Soldotna. The female students, along with Dean of Women Eva Oyoumick, lived in one part of the house while the 11 male students lived in the pool room—with rows of bunk beds lined up along the walls. It was affectionately known as "the petri dish."

Siemers eventually moved into the second floor of one of the new cabins (Arvada Cabin) built on campus by volunteers. The heater—as well as the kitchen and bathroom—were both on the first floor, where a married couple later lived, while the second floor was unheated. There was a hatch leading up the second where heat was supposed to come through, but it was closed most of the time to give his housemates their privacy. A sink and a bathroom were later installed on the second floor, but by then, Siemers had moved out.

Eventually, male students moved to cabins of their own, while the female students stayed in the main building. Things were cramped, Siemers recalled, but everyone got by.

When the school started, there was one classroom, which all the instructors shared, while the students all had the same class schedule of courses. For most of the early staff, working at the college was life as much as a job—and their role was not just to teach or to administer programs, but also to create a living, breathing community. Fortunately, adjunct professors jumped in to carry some of the teaching load, like Rev. Scott Pitsch, a Covenant pastor from Anchorage, who would later move his family to Kenai and serve the students for 20 plus years in a variety of roles.

Siemers said that in the early days, it was not clear that the college would survive. But those kinds of long-term questions weren't the focus. Instead, the staff, faculty, and volunteers threw themselves into the work and focused on the task at hand. That was the important part, said Siemers.

"I think it came down to the point where I didn't care," he said. "I think it was more about meeting the students where they were and finding a place for them."

Alan Finifrock, who ended up taking on a great deal of the day-to-day administration while Hamilton was out raising funds, echoed that feeling. He told the college's archivist, that creating a supportive Christian community became essential to the college's identity. Creating a sense of trust and security took time, he said, but it was what students needed.

"The most important thing for this school was to present or offer a safe place for students to get away from home and grow up," he said. "Discipleship helped them connect with other kids in a safe setting."

The staff also spent time finding creative ways to engage students outside of the classroom. For Finifrock, this meant setting up an ice rink on the campus, which hosted broomball games through the winter months. The students would eventually compete for the "Finifrock Cup"—an old plastic trophy wrapped in foil—which infused friendly competition and building into the broomball competition.

Hamilton and other staffers also focused on the positive. Nineteen students returned after that Christmas break, which Hamilton saw as a sign of success. A MIRACLE! Some of the students who returned had told staff they were not going back—and yet there they were. Other students, who knew they might not show the academic progress needed to graduate, still wanted to stay and be part of the Christian community, an option offered by the college. Those students would get the Certificate of Participation at the end of the year.

By the start of the spring quarter, the school's finances began to improve. The funds from the Murdock Trust were in the bank and the school was solvent enough to be able to put some funds into reserves. Hamilton and the board began to turn their gaze toward the future.

On the staffing side, leaders at ACC knew they needed to recruit more female staffers to balance out the faculty and staff, where most of the key leaders were men, while half of the students were women. This led to the school hiring Dr. Cheryl Davis (now Siemers after marrying Jeff), who had a Ph.D. and experience in higher education as a professor and director of development. Davis had been a professor at Cedarville, a Christian college in Ohio, and had spent time at ACC in the fall of 2001 while on sabbatical. That experience, Hamilton believed, made her the right person to help the school, as she understood the college's mission and culture. She also had the academic expertise to serve as academic dean and an instructor.

The school also had small signs that things were going to be all right. By the end of March, funds were tight and it was unclear that the college would make payroll by March 31. Phyllis Mickelson, who had been the volunteer secretary since the opening of ACC, and her husband, Bob, were leaving ACC to move back to Washington State. Hamilton asked Sharon Finifrock if she would assist at the front desk in the interim period until a new person could be found. With $7,000 needed to make payroll on the last day of the month, the safe was empty. Praying for a miracle that would come in the mail that day, Sharon waited for the mail and also began to look through the files at the desk. When the mail came, nothing came for the college. While digging through the files to acquaint herself with the system, Sharon opened up a closed manila folder. Upon opening it, she discovered an envelope full of checks that were three months old that had never been cashed, totaling just over $7,000 in checks that had yet to be deposited. A MIRACLE!

Meanwhile, interest in the college seemed to be growing, and by April, 44 students had applied for the fall of 2002—with hopes that as many as 34 students might end up attending, which would be the school's maximum capacity. That spring, the school also hosted a retreat called Uiñiq that brought 20 students from Alaska churches to campus, allowing them to get a firsthand look at what ACC had to offer.

At the end of April, 18 students prepared to walk across the stage at the college's first commencement. It was a bittersweet time, as staffers had seen how much the students had grown while knowing how many challenges they still faced.

"We are deeply concerned about their futures, so much that we are now considering a full second-year program to accommodate the few that would benefit from that ministry," Hamilton wrote, as graduation approached. "We are concerned that just as we began to see some students turn the corner, we released them too early to function in stability that is only found where deep roots are planted. I cannot change our mission, but we can change how we go about it."

Finally, graduation day arrived, with parents and families eager to cheer their students on.

After a Saturday night banquet, the student choir sang for their families as part of an evening worship service. The next morning, about 85 people packed in and gathered for worship in the Denali Room, followed by another meal, then the president held a reception where parents had a chance to meet with the staff.

"We heard the hearts of pain and gladness from each parent present," Hamilton later recalled.

Then it was off to Peninsula Grace Church, where students in full caps and gowns received their certificates to the cheers of the assembled crowd. Gail Smithhisler, one of the students, gave her testimony, and at the end, her mother came on stage to embrace her. A moving moment!

During the service, Hamilton handed out eight full diplomas to graduates and another 10 certificates of partial completion to other students who still had work to do. During the service, as they came on stage, each of the students handed Hamilton a paperclip—a sign of appreciation and thanks for all he and the staff had done, and a bit of an inside joke. Hamilton had been fond of saying that the college had started with not even a paperclip—and look how far they had come. Mark Hill put them up to it!

"I will keep these forever," Hamilton would later write in his journal, summing up all that he felt in that moment. Today, they hang in his office next to his desk as a reminder of God's provision.

In the week approaching graduation, one of the students, Donald Fancher, approached the staff with a question. He had hoped to attend Kenai Peninsula College, whose Kenai River campus lay about a quarter of a mile away from the ACC campus. Hamilton told him he couldn't stay a second year as ACC was a one-year program only. Donald asked again if he could stay at ACC and just take classes at KPC, as they had no student housing. So, he became the first student to spend a second year at ACC, and the decision to allow him to stay would have long-term implications, eventually helping open the door for ACC to be accredited. The name "Encore Program" was given to this program. It meant that they could "repeat a performance" by coming back! Another student, George Sookiyak, also remained on campus most of the summer working and serving alongside volunteers. He became what is known today as an ACC Ambassador.

"This is a trial using ACC and Kenai Peninsula College as the institutions together offering classes with a two-year Bible and General Studies Certificate," Hamilton recorded in his journal after the staff unanimously voted to move forward with Fancher's request, which would subsequently be approved by the board. The plan was for Fancher to earn an associate degree from KPC while attending classes at both schools. In the end, Fancher would graduate from KPC and then North Park University with a teaching credential and returned to his native village of Unalakleet to teach there. A MIRACLE!

The college ended the school year with $230,000 in the bank, with an extra $10,000 arriving to help with ongoing operation expenses at the very end. A MIRACLE!

"What a great group of servants our staff represents, in the eyes of the Lord, and my eyes," Hamilton wrote in summing up the first year. "I am amazed at what we have done all together for His Kingdom here in Alaska."

After graduation, the staff bid goodbye not just to the students but also to Paul Wilson, who had decided to leave Alaska for a local church pastorate at First Covenant Church in Oakland, California. There, he would remain a vocal supporter and do some consulting work, but would no longer be in a leadership role at the school.

The summer of 2002 brought a whirlwind of activity to campus, as the staff began to prepare for more work groups to arrive. The first major project was getting the permits and foundation for a new duplex in place, which proved trickier due to a mix-up with the fire marshal's office. Volunteers Bob Bode and Dave Alexander, with the help of students, got the foundation poured, while Dave Isaak from the Soldotna Bible Chapel helped get the site ready.

After a trip to the Covenant's annual meeting in Colorado in late June, where the work of ACC was acknowledged by Rev. Glenn Palmberg, the denomination's president, Hamilton returned to campus with work still to be done on the duplex. This would house female students in the fall with the help of another work crew from Arvada Covenant. This church remains the most faithful in sending teams to ACC over its history.

While construction went forward, funds for the ongoing work of the college proved harder to come by. Hamilton, like many fundraisers, had learned that raising funds for designated projects like duplexes could be easier than the ongoing work of raising funds for operations. So while funding for the duplex and other projects was in place, and some long-term funding for staff roles, the college would have ongoing cash flow issues. It now needed $11,000 in donations and an additional $10,000 in a personal loan to make payroll and pay other expenses.

"With the building fund getting down to the bottom, we can only finish that which we have funds for," Hamilton recorded in his journal. "No loans or borrowing against the other accounts as before. I pray we can finish the duplex and maintenance building as we need them both badly."

Bringing Dr. Cheryl Davis on board as Director of Development meant a second person was working on raising funds for the college and she spent much of that first summer working on grant proposals. The major task went to the Murdock Trust again, in hopes of getting $500,000 to build a new residence hall that would expand the school's long-term capacity and help make the school viable in the long term.

That summer, 59 students applied to start school in the fall. But staff hopes that as many as thirty students might arrive on campus would likely fall short. As long as the school had more than 20 students, things would work out financially. Still, there were difficult decisions to make, especially when students lacked the finances to attend the college.

"When in youth ministry, I would never turn someone away because of finances. I had a whole church behind me there," Hamilton wrote in his journal toward the end of the summer. "Here I have no backing like that and must watch how much free tuition we give out.... It is hard to turn anyone down because we know that God may be leading them here."

Before school started that fall, the college received more news. First, the leadership learned that Dan Thornton, a local pastor who had served as the college's choir director, had to drop out right before classes started. There were also issues with plumbing at the duplex, leading to major repairs which left the building without water as the students were ready to move in. Thankfully, a donor stepped up to pay for the repairs, meaning only a few waterless days for the students in the duplex.

By September, 22 new students arrived on campus, joined by Fancher and another second-year student named Wilma. Six of the students were American Indian young people from the lower 48, joined by two First Nations Canadians and a pair of white students; one from Wisconsin, the other from California. The remaining dozen students were Alaska Native.

The year began with hopes for the success of the program. If Donald were to graduate at the end of the year with a certificate in something ACC had to offer, then the college could be able to apply for the first step toward accreditation with the Association for Biblical Higher Education (ABHE). Doing that would allow students to qualify for state and federal financial aid and would help ACC standardize its enrollment process, which until this point, had been largely built on the fly.

With a year under their belt, the staff was better prepared to welcome students. Those students also seemed more mature and ready for college.

"This is a very connected class already, and seem to immediately show more responsibility and care for each other and their schoolwork," Hamilton recounted in his journal. "We are all amazed at their eagerness, attentiveness, and desire to grow and learn. We, as a staff, are just so much more prepared this year than last. We are so ahead of where we were last year with the dedication, the opening day, the 9/11 disaster, and having never done this college thing before."

In preparation for year two, the college had beefed up its counseling services, with both Debbie Hamilton and Kristi Ivanoff available to meet with students as counselors. There were also hopes of eventually adding more services if funding could become available. And despite being more prepared than the previous year, students still faced significant challenges in adapting to life at college. In some ways, ACC was ahead of the curve in dealing with the mental health challenges that college students face, because of the population the school knew it was serving.

In October of 2003, the Hamiltons made their way to Washington, DC to meet with senior staff from U.S. Senators Lisa Murkowski and Ted Steven's offices, as well as Congressman Don Young's office, in hopes of finding funding for a new residence hall. They would soon learn that funding for a residence hall was unlikely but funding for a counseling center was more promising.

"Keith was looking for funding under any rock," Debbie recalled in a 2024 interview. "We were sharing this vision of this fledgling, brand-new college that wanted to help young adults from western Alaska."

During a meeting, a longtime staffer for then-Alaskan U.S. Senator Ted Stevens, told the Hamiltons that there was no funding available for student housing after Hamilton showed her a postcard from the senator proclaiming he was pro-Bush Alaska (defined as rural Alaska, off the road system). However, there was federal funding available for counseling. On the spot, she asked the Hamiltons to come up with a proposal for a grant that would eventually fund the New Hope Counseling Center, an essential part of Alaska Christian College's story.

"I always say that I went along as the tagalong wife, to go see the monuments and for a great trip, and came home with a grant for a counseling center," Debbie Hamilton said in a 2024 interview. When asked for the name of the counseling center, without hesitation, she stated, "New Hope Counseling Center." Keith came home empty-handed without funds for the residence hall.

The process took a bit longer. After submitting the grant, Debbie began working on plans for what the counseling center could be. Then in early 2004, her cellphone rang while she was pumping gas, with three kids in the car. On the other end was a staff member from U.S. Senator Lisa Murkowski's office.

"Hey, we're just really excited about what's happening down in Soldotna and the work that you're doing there, and we just want to let you know that you've been awarded a $200,000 grant for your counseling project," Debbie recalled the staffer saying. "I was just speechless." A MIRACLE!

The grant was part of an earmark through SAMHSA, the Substance Abuse Mental Health Services Administration. That funding proved essential, allowing the college to fund needed support services and eventually to start a counseling center that would serve students as well as the community.

The idea of the center was to be proactive, Debbie Hamilton said, and to provide services to students early on, rather than waiting until a student was in crisis. It was part of the school's whole-life approach to education. But getting students to take advantage of the counseling and support of the school was a complicated puzzle. The students often came to school from communities with significant levels of substance abuse, domestic violence, and suicide rates—and had often experienced trauma.

"We had a student the very first year at ACC who knew over 20 family members who had taken their lives," she said. "It was mind-blowing—just the sense of despair and hopelessness."

To cope with that trauma, the students themselves had often turned to alcohol or other substances, putting them at odds with college rules for community life and leading at times to self-destructive behaviors. That led the college leaders to address the root causes that led students to self-medicate with alcohol.

"That's the number one coping strategy for stress, disillusionment and pain, and loss," Debbie Hamilton said. "We are trying to resource them in other ways of coping beyond substance abuse."

On top of the trauma they may have experienced, the students were also experiencing significant life change—leaving what often were small, tightly knit communities where traditional ways of Alaska Native culture were still cherished, and diving headlong into the noise and busyness of modern life. The first step in that process of helping students make that transition is often just helping students feel safe and providing a supportive environment where they can let down their guard and begin to tell their stories. They are not used to the road system and even seeing so many trees. Many trips are made those first weeks to the beaches nearby.

"ACC is very relational," said Debbie Hamilton. "And that in and of itself becomes a healing environment—to be in a place where you begin to feel safe or you have people that sit and listen."

Like many young people, students at ACC are also trying to figure out the story of their own lives and what their future will look like. Part of that is growing spiritually and getting a sense of what God's calling might be for them—while learning academic skills, adjusting to living on their own away from family, and making plans for their future.

Receiving the funds for the counseling center was a turning point for the college, a first step toward some much-needed financial stability. The grant would also eventually become nationwide news, as the college had unknowingly taken a first step into the long-brewing battles over the separation of church and state that comes with any government funding for faith-based groups.

In the meantime, the college still struggled to make payroll and to cover the costs of building projects. ACC now needed $6,500 to pay off a credit card account used to buy materials. Cash flow remained an ongoing concern, often sending Keith Hamilton out on what he called "the potluck trail" of speaking at churches and telling the college's story in an effort to raise financial support.

There were also staffing challenges. College leaders were left trying to fill key support roles in the kitchen and in maintenance especially. Calls went out to invite anyone who could come and volunteer for a season or a lifetime.

Finding the right person to serve as a cook remained a challenge. With a couple dozen students and a shoestring budget, the college wasn't able to pay more than minimum wage for a cook. And being new, the college staff had few contacts in the community for recruiting new staff.

Eventually, a staff member passed on the name Gary Hanley, who had been a cook at the Kenai Princess Lodge that catered to tourists and had been laid off at the end of the summer season, who might be a good fit. Hanley, who was then looking after his young daughter at home, had a side business already—but still was open to part-time work to supplement his income, said Sharon Finifrock.

"He was wonderful," said Finifrock. "He knew how to buy for a commercial kitchen. He knew how to utilize leftovers. He made wonderful soups—and Keith loves soups, so that was a plus. He also knew how to budget. He was just what we needed."

Despite many challenges, along the way there was always progress. That fall, the college's board approved a two-year Certificate of Biblical and General Studies for Encore students like Donald, the title of the new program that allowed students to study at ACC for a year and then receive this certificate after attending a second year of classes at nearby Kenai Peninsula College. The new plan to make ACC a two-option educational program was solidified. A MIRACLE!

That decision made it possible for ACC to apply for accreditation through the Association for Biblical Higher Education (ABHE), which would allow students to be eligible for financial aid in the future, as well as open up access to other federal funding for education. When considering accreditation, there were only two accrediting agencies in the United States approved by the U.S. Department of Education that served Bible colleges. One was located in Virginia and one in

Orlando, Florida. Guess which one Hamilton contacted first? On that late-night call to the ABHE offices at the end of the second year, Hamilton connected with Dr. Randy Bell, their accreditation guru. After a long list of all the requirements to just apply for accreditation, the key factor and requirement was that ACC had at least *one* graduate of a two-year program. Thanks to the perseverance of Donald Fancher, ACC had just *one*! A MIRACLE!

"This is a major task, but well worth the process for the benefit potential," Hamilton wrote in his journal after the meeting. "There could come a day when we could afford to charge closer to the cost of ACC's education and have more students to disciple. This is truly enhancing our ministry of 'whole-life' discipleship."

Board members also approved phase one of a planned 28-bed dormitory to house students. This building would be called "Quyana" or "thank you" in Yup'ik. The whole project would cost an estimated $700,000, with an initial $34,250 needed for start-up work like hiring an architect for the project and digging a well needed to provide water for the entire campus. Hamilton hoped that the Murdock Trust would help support the project long term. In the short term, four teams of volunteers had signed up to begin work the following summer.

Along with leading the college, Hamilton took a role as Volunteer Captain at Central Emergency Services, the local fire department, which put him in charge of working with about 35 volunteer firefighters. Hamilton had been trained as an EMT and after arriving in Soldotna, began work as a volunteer firefighter and EMT, in 2001. This promotion brought new responsibilities as well as a source of income when things got tight at the college with payroll. There were many times that the president was the last to be paid, even well into the new month. This role also often allowed him to serve as a chaplain, ministering in the community when tragedy struck, and to bring mercy and grace to people facing impossible difficulties. Hamilton continues to serve the community in this way and has done so since 1978, beginning at age 16.

By the end of the year, the college had caught up on all its bills and began to see funds roll in for the new year, including about $31,000 for building and operations that showed up as part of the college's end-of-year giving program. The college also received a donated snowplow from Six Robblees and a donation toward the purchase of a 1995 Ford Club Cab pickup. That winter was unusually light in snow and the truck and plow were used only once!

In early 2003, Hamilton turned his focus to the residence hall project. Richard Borgeson, a volunteer architect from Forest Park Covenant Church in Muskegon, Michigan, traveled to Alaska to go over the blueprints for the project and to help with planning. During that time together, it became clear that the college would have to find an on-site supervisor for the project, one with more skill than the college had on hand, as well as being a volunteer general contractor. Jim Engwall, who had volunteered with ACC in development, suggested a man from First Covenant Church in Rockford, Illinois, named Dick Nelson. Dick had spent 40 summers serving in construction in many of the Covenant's villages in western Alaska and was ready for the new challenge.

The college also received a $150,000 donation for the new dormitory from a very generous Arvada family, which would add $100,000 in promised donations from work crews scheduled that summer. If a hoped-for gift of $45,000 from a Covenant church came in, most of the dorm project would be partially funded before its construction began. A MIRACLE!

Then it was May again and another commencement. Ten graduates of the one-year Bible Certificate program, and another eight received Certificates of Participation for the year. Don Fancher became the school's first two-year graduate with a Certificate in General and Biblical Studies, another enormous step forward for the college. A MIRACLE!

"Commencement has come and gone—another holy time for all involved with parents and families all coming to celebrate the amazing stories of our year together," Hamilton wrote in his journal to sum up the experience.

The next few months were filled with construction projects, meetings, and worries about money as the college's new residence hall began to take shape. Hamilton returned to the campus after several weeks away from vacation and meetings to find the three-story hall already framed out and moving forward, thanks to the oversight of Dick Nelson and a team from Faith in Action Ministries from Appleton, Wisconsin. That group was followed by a team from First Covenant Church in Rockford IL, along with other electricians and plumbers who gave their time to the project.

As the building went up, the college received a visitor from the Murdock Trust who toured the campus and got a firsthand look at the college. That visit brought hopes that the Trust might help fund the completion cost of the dorm project. The Murdock staff also invited Hamilton to a leadership roundtable, part of their investment in helping nonprofits build capacity and skills. The visit was timely, as the college once again had run short of funds, due in part because of cost overruns in the dorm project such as installing an expensive sprinkler system.

During this time, Hamilton and other leaders were also grappling with the ongoing challenge of how to support students, given that only about half the students had graduated during the college's first two years. They worried about how to balance the educational needs of students—and their needs for emotional and spiritual growth. Hamilton began to consider offering an audit track for students who wanted to grow spiritually but did not have the academic skills yet to succeed in college. At the same time, the staff was focused on preparing to become an accredited institution, a process that would take nine years, the fastest track possible according to ABHE.

The summer ended with meetings with government officials, first in Washington, DC, to discuss the grant for the counseling center, then with the Department of Education about funding for the Encore Program, which could cover staff and other ongoing costs. There were also meetings with Southcentral Foundation, an Alaska Native nonprofit, about funding for the college, as well as calls with staffers from Congressman Don Young's office about a possible $400,000 grant.

"How is it that the federal government can give tax dollars to a Christian college? While I don't understand it, I trust God for it," Hamilton would write in his journal, in a question that occupied his mind and the minds of many around the country, especially the U.S. Department of Education, in the years to come.

While there was great promise in the long-term sustainability for the college, the day-to-day issues remained challenging. So much so, it was unclear by the end of each month whether the college would make payroll and keep the lights on. As was true from the beginning, the school was held together by shoestrings and miracles— where the one constant has been change.

"You are always dependent on the Lord," Debbie Hamilton said in a 2024 interview, reflecting on the college history. "Because you never feel like you're in a fully sustainable model."

The Hamilton family was called from Arvada, Colorado to Soldotna, Alaska in November 2000.

First view of the 8400 square foot house on Royal Place in January 2001.

Official signing of the mortgage for the future home of Alaska Christian College.

2001-02 team of mission staff, adjuncts, and volunteers.

First three cabins completed for men's housing in November 2001; named the Arvada, Castle Oaks, and Shawnee cabins.

Housing duplex, completed in 2002, named the Iron Mountain and N. Mankato units; soon to become the first New Hope Counseling Center office.

New sign at the entrance to Royal Place, built by volunteers in 2002.

First graduating class of 18 students in May 2002.

Construction of Quyana Residence Hall began in 2003.

Quyana Residence Hall, housing up to 35 residents, completed in November 2003.

The Quyana Residence Hall was dedicated in 2003. Volunteer contractor, Dick Nelson, from Rockford, Illinois, oversaw this building project.

The start of construction on the Peninsula Conference Center dining hall in 2007.

Peninsula Conference Center completed in 2009 and able to accommodate up to 150 guests and students.

Aerial view of campus in 2008.

New Hope Counseling Center (Forest Park building) opened in 2009 to serve both students and community members.

Sports shack completed in 2009.

The ACC men's intramural team won 2nd place in the Kenai Recreation Center B-League in 2009.

The ACC choir sang at the Native Musicale in Anchorage.

Jimmy Andrew graduated in 2006 and went on to become a teacher with a Master's degree serving in Bush Alaska.

ACC graduate, Rae Fancher, became the first female Alaska Native to graduate from the United States Naval Academy in 2010.

The student choir toured throughout Alaska during the first year.

ACC received accreditation through the Association for Biblical Higher Education in February 2012.

5

By the fall of 2004, the college seemed to be finally reaching a place of stability, for now.

In September of that year, 37 students arrived on campus, including 10 in the Encore program, taking classes at nearby Kenai Peninsula College, making it the largest enrollment in the school's three-year history and a rebound from 2003, when only 15 new students enrolled. The Encore program also seemed to be a success—with double-digit enrollment for the second year in a row, showing that some students were making the kind of progress that the college's founders had hoped for. A MIRACLE!

While not flush with cash, the college finances had stabilized, in large part due to an influx of funds from the federal government which included a $400,000 grant from the U.S. Department of Education facilitated by Alaska's sole U.S. Representative, Don Young. The original grant request had been made for student housing—but after consulting with a staff member in Congressman Young's office, the request had been reconfigured to pay for a dining hall, scholarships, recruiting, staff salaries, and other costs. Those funds, along with the $200,000 for the New Hope Counseling Center, had proven to be a godsend. And there was hope for additional funds for the future. A MIRACLE!

A year earlier, the picture had been less promising. Only two dozen students had arrived on campus, leaving the brand-new residence hall only half full. The dorm, which opened that fall, still lacked heating and a sprinkler system, and the building fund was empty. While the college had been awarded a major grant from the Murdock Trust to complete the building, those funds had yet to arrive. The school still needed to raise $20,000 in matching funds to free up the remaining portion of a previous Murdock grant.

Because of the low enrollment, the college's already-thin budget was cut by $50,000 and once again, the college was looking for a miracle and relying on faith as the year began—with Hamilton out on the road raising funds to keep things going.

By the end of the year, things were looking up. The college had finally reached the matching funds mark for the first Murdock grant, freeing up $75,000 in funds that had been previously frozen. The New Hope Counseling Center had 18 clients, and their work was beginning to bear fruit—and the funding from the federal government for the counseling services provided much-needed revenue back to the college.

While running the college at home and raising funds mainly outside Alaska, Hamilton had a medical situation that would slow him down. Six months prior he had surgery and, unfortunately, it was done incorrectly, and now, in early December, he landed in the hospital for an extended stay following surgery for Zenker's diverticulum—a condition that affected his esophagus. Complications from the second surgery and a staph infection led to two more surgeries while he was at Providence Hospital in Anchorage.

"I spent two weeks lying in a hospital bed and don't recall most of it. I lived on morphine," he would later write in his journal. "My doctor came in twice daily to move me toward wellness, but it took the healing prayers of God's people to restore me." Friends would later tell him and show him the crazy emails he was sending from his bed that made no sense.

Hamilton also faced a crisis in 2004, when the challenges that students faced, on top of the daily difficulties of keeping the college going, seemed to be too much. Other students were struggling with mental illness, alcohol, and what seemed like an ongoing string of unexpected pregnancies among students who were unprepared for the responsibilities of parenting. Many of the students were also unable to pay their tuition, leaving the college with nearly $100,000 in anticipated tuition revenue that might never come in. There seemed to be more failure than success—and growth and maturity among the students was slow in coming. The college had taken on what seemed to be an impossible task and the reality that all could turn downward seemed to be closing in.

The discouragement Hamilton felt led him to reach out to Rev. Rodney Sawyer, who had succeeded Paul Wilson as Alaska's Covenant Church Field Director, about getting support through the Covenant's Sustaining Pastoral Excellence program, and eventually, to seek out more education that might help him in his role as ACC president. In his journals, he wrote about his struggles and about the support he felt from family during that time, which also acknowledged that any time he spent at home meant he was not raising funds. For a time, he was caught between a rock and a hard place, knowing that he needed to rest and yet knowing resting meant the college could fall behind. Again, he needed to fully trust and rely upon the Lord.

By the end of January, Hamilton's health had returned and an additional $150,000 SAMHSA grant was approved by Congress and signed by then-President Bush. Another major request was submitted to the Murdock Trust for other campus needs. This Trust has been a major pillar in ACC's ongoing story of fulfilling its mission over the past 25 years.

In February, the Hamiltons and Dr. Cheryl Davis, the Academic Dean and Development Director, made their way to Florida for the annual meeting of the Association for Biblical Higher Education, where they learned that ACC had been approved as an applicant for accreditation, the start of a four-year process toward initial accreditation, a major step forward. A MIRACLE!

A few weeks later, Dale Solberg, a college librarian from Minnesota, traveled to ACC to investigate volunteering for a period of time. He agreed to join the staff by volunteering from a distance, beginning immediately, and with the plan to move to Alaska temporarily and live on campus and volunteer for the 2004-2005 school year to help oversee the accreditation process—which would turn out to be a huge boon.

The year ended with 13 first-year students graduating, along with two of the Encore students. Alaska Lieutenant Governor Loren Leman, Alaska's first Indigenous executive branch leader, served as the commencement speaker, while

Ryan Mute, Bea Katongan, and Sylvia Sheldon were honored as students of the year. Loren Leman is currently serving on the Board of Trustees.

That summer was subdued, with few work crews and work on the new dining hall limited to putting in a new foundation for the project—a reminder that despite the federal grants, the school's finances often were a challenge. The end of the summer also meant saying goodbye to Mark and Joanna Hill, who were headed off to North Park Theological Seminary.

Highlights from that fall included a visit from a staff member from Congressman Young's office, who toured the campus and met with students to hear about the impact of state-funded scholarships. The staff member had been instrumental in arranging the initial $400,000 grant and a follow-up $435,000 grant, which was approved by Congress that November, meaning the college had received about a million dollars in federal funding in a relatively short period of time.

The first sign that the grants might cause trouble for the college came in early 2005 when a front-page story critical of the grants appeared in the *Anchorage Daily News*. The story was followed a few days later by a searing editorial that accused lawmakers of violating the separation of church and state—and dismissing the work of the college as religious indoctrination.

"Alaska's congressional delegation might just as well have put a $1 million check in the church collection plate," the editorial read.

The college's response to the story, which Hamilton described as "not very positive"—was mostly silence. The hope was that after a few days, any furor over the story would die down and college leaders decided to follow the adage that "any publicity is good publicity," reasoning now that readers across the state would now be aware of the college's work.

"We are also well-known in Alaska with people still commenting about the front-page article in *Anchorage Daily News*," Hamilton wrote in his journal, commenting that the school's reputation has spread not just through the Covenant denomination but also across the State of Alaska. "We still have not received any negative feedback from anyone directly to ACC."

However, the article caught the attention of the Freedom From Religion Foundation, an activist group from Madison, Wisconsin, that fiercely opposed any government funding of religious groups. In April of 2005, the group filed a lawsuit against the Department of Education in the U.S. District Court for the Western District of Wisconsin, seeking to freeze any government funds not yet disbursed to the college and to block any further grants to ACC and other religious schools.

"The actions of the defendant in dispersing Congressional taxpayer appropriations to endorse and advance religion violate the Establishment Clause of the First Amendment to the United States Constitution, including as a result of the failure to assure that funded educational programs, such as the Alaska Christian College, do not substantively incorporate religion," lawyers for the foundation wrote in the complaint filed in federal court.

The lawsuit made headlines across the country and made ACC the focus of a long-running national dispute over the relationship between religion and politics.

"It has no purpose except to proselytize. It is not, truly, a college. It doesn't even offer Math or English," Annie Laurie Gaylor, the FFRF's co-president told *The Washington Post*.

While admitting that ACC had a Christian mission, Hamilton pointed out to reporters like those at the Post that the college had secular benefits in helping Native students make the transition from high school to college.

"It's essentially a Christian college, not a Bible school," Hamilton told the Post. "Bible schools traditionally only teach Bible courses. We're broader than that, teaching much more."

Ironically, the college received a notice from the Department of Education saying that it could start spending funds from the $435,000 grant a few days after learning about the lawsuit. Hamilton also received a call from Alliance Defending Freedom, a nonprofit group that promotes the free exercise of religion, who often found itself at odds with groups like the FFRF, where Hamilton learned that the lawsuit would likely lead to a long court case.

Inadvertently, the college had become part of an ongoing conflict over how best to interpret the First Amendment's guidance about religion and its role in public life. While barring the United States from an official state church, the Constitution also makes it clear that the government could not interfere with the free exercise of religion. That had led in recent years to fierce battles in the courts over how to best apply the First Amendment to religion in public life, especially where public money is concerned.

The lawsuit was part of a larger pattern of legal challenges to President George W. Bush's faith-based initiative, which sought to expand the ways that religious nonprofits and the government could work together to address social problems. That led to legal challenges over government grants to groups like the Salvation Army and Prison Fellowship and put groups like the FFRF on the lookout for grants to religious groups as targets for future lawsuits, *The Washington Post* would report in the fall of 2005.

The weak part of the faith-based initiative, Robert Tuttle, a George Washington University law professor, told the Post, was a "lack of clarity about what the government may or may not fund." Suits like the one challenging the ACC grants would help bring clarity to that question, which was little comfort. Losing access to government funds would be a hardship for the college and the lawsuit would overshadow much of the college's work for the next year.

"ACC can surely survive, but our student services would be drastically reduced and scholarships almost non-existent," Hamilton wrote in his journal. "I am praying for wisdom and God to give us peace in this storm. We have done nothing wrong; we asked, we received, we spent, and now someone is trying to take this away from us. We will pray."

The college also found itself caught in a broader conversation over religion and ethnicity, especially when it comes to how religious groups and the federal government have treated Native people in the United States. The FFRF described the government grants as part of an effort to convert Alaska Natives to Christianity, which college leaders felt ignored the role that Native church leaders in Alaska had played in founding the college.

"The question is whether the government can fund religion with no holds barred, no strings attached," Gaylor, co-president of the FFRF, told Inside Higher Education, a publication focused on the national policy and the inner workings of the nation's colleges and universities. "This is an attempt to proselytize Native Americans and offer them an inferior education at massive taxpayer expense."

National politics, especially over earmarks—often inserted into national bills at the request of legislators like Alaska senators and congressmen—also drew attention to the conflict over the grants, as did the fact that the college was not yet accredited.

ACC found itself in the middle of a perfect storm, turning its grants into ongoing national headlines.

"Some experts bemoan the trend toward earmarks, contending that the money is now granted according to connections rather than merit," the Post reported, in giving context to the lawsuit over the ACC grant. "Lawmakers say they know constituents' needs better than officials in Washington."

That left Hamilton and other college leaders in both a public relations and legal battle, often feeling like they were fighting an uphill battle. Part of the challenge that the college was facing was that while the mission of the school was motivated and shaped by faith—and funded mostly by churches and other faith-based donors—the idea of "whole-life discipleship" had broad social, emotional, and educational implications.

"There are emotional, intellectual, spiritual, physical, and social components in people's lives," Hamilton told Inside Higher Ed, in a story reporting about the controversy over the grants. "ACC's mission is to give students opportunities to grow in each of these areas through mentoring, academics, tutoring, career assessment, Bible learning, Native community, and counseling."

While courts have long allowed federal funding for religious colleges, as long as that funding went to reach secular subjects, direct funding for religious goals was seen differently, Douglas Laycock, a national expert on the First Amendment told Inside Higher Ed, while discussing the ACC case. The Christian focus of ACC likely would work against the college in the FFRF lawsuit, Laycock told the publication.

But there was hope. The key would be whether or not the courts would see enough secular benefit to the college's work to allow the grants to stand. Richard W. Garnett, an associate professor of law at the University of Notre Dame, saw some hope for that—especially, he told the Chronicle, if the courts believed that the goal of assisting Native students to succeed in college was a secular and not just a religious aim.

Still, the college faced an uphill battle.

"We are going to stand on the truth of who we are and try to make sure our story, what ACC truly is, becomes a consistent message," Hamilton wrote in his journal. "I realize that we are in a battle bigger than life and I am praying that I do not get discouraged nor worn down as I attempt to serve here with minimal distractions."

There were some benefits from the lawsuit. *The Peninsula Clarion*, a local paper, showed up at graduation for a feature story on Travis Tutt, one of 27 students who took part in the ceremony, including 13 first-year graduates and one second-year graduate.

"Today again proved to me why I am committed to ACC and will not give up the fight for the students," Hamilton would later write in his journal.

In response to the lawsuit, college leaders slashed the school's budget by $400,000 and cut back on spending. They hoped that at least the college would be able to keep the funds it had already spent and not have to pay them back.

Meanwhile, there was more good news. Donations to the college still rolled in, showing that support among churches remained strong and Hamilton was encouraged by the reception he received at the Covenant denomination's annual meeting, where supporters expressed their concerns about the effect of the lawsuit on the school.

After the Covenant annual meeting, Hamilton made his way to Minneapolis to visit donors and friends. He also officiated at the wedding of Dale Solberg and Lois Link—a couple in their 50s who were soon to play an important role together at the college. Dale had taken an unpaid leave of absence from the University of Northwestern and lived on campus at ACC while volunteering from September 2004–May 2005, and continued volunteering from a distance until he and Lois moved to Alaska in December 2005. Dale began serving as an administrative faculty member, bringing with him experience with the accreditation process for colleges. He would play a crucial role in helping the college manage that process for the next twelve years.

Hamilton returned to campus to meet with Derek Gaubatz, the director of litigation for the Becket Fund, a Washington, DC–based nonprofit that focused on religious freedom cases. Becket had agreed to represent the college on a pro-bono basis and help them navigate the complexities of the case—even if the college was not a party to the lawsuit, the outcome of the suit would have a long-term impact on the college's future.

In particular, Gaubatz helped the college prepare for a site visit from a program director for the U.S. Department of Education, who would be evaluating the college's program as part of the government's response to the lawsuit. Gaubatz also met with the college's accountant and Hamilton, advising on the kind of changes to the budget that would likely be required because of the lawsuit. Gaubatz also took over the role of speaking to the press, using his interviews to defend the college in the media.

Hamilton, for his part, believed the college would be all right in the end. "I believe our honesty and integrity will win in the long battle, maybe not the short skirmishes, but we stand strong and ready," he wrote in his journal, after the U.S. Department of Education visit, which went fairly well.

In the short term, the college would likely need an infusion of cash to pay its bills if the government funds were frozen. As part of the suit, the FFRF had filed for an injunction to block the school from spending any of the $435,000 from the second Department of Education grant, which was likely to be granted. That left the college needing to raise between $250,000 and $300,000 to pay its bills over the coming year—a need that Hamilton outlined in a letter to donors.

By the time students arrived back on campus that fall—20 first-year students, 10 second-year students, and one student back for a third year—the Department of Education had frozen the grant funds, including $50,000 the college had planned to use for scholarships. In addition, Hamilton received a subpoena to be deposed in the case.

While classes began, lawyers from Becket and the federal government discussed how the lawsuit would proceed, with the expectation that the government would settle the suit. The main question appeared to be, how much of the funds might still be available to ACC once all the dust had settled? In the meantime, the college experienced a successful summer, with 225 volunteers from 15 different church work teams coming to the campus to work on the new dining hall. However, the project was shut down in August, with the building fund out of money and a potential funding crisis looming.

By Labor Day, Gaubatz called with the news that the lawsuit had been settled. The gist of the settlement was that the college would *not* have to repay any funds, which was good news. A MIRACLE! The bad news was that the second grant would remain frozen for the time being, with the college given time to submit a new budget to spend the funds on non-religious line items. But doing so came with a risk.

"We are starting from scratch and the FFRF could sue the Department of Education again," Hamilton recalled in his journal after getting the news, adding that he believed the White House's faith-based office had played a role in settling the case in a way that left the door open for the college to use the grant funds in the future.

In a letter to the college, a Department of Education staff member said the college had not put "adequate safeguards" in place to differentiate between secular and religious activities, and that students had been required to take part in religious activities. This was not entirely true, as ACC had never required students to attend chapel, church, or Bible studies, for example.

"Moreover, we have concluded that the College has used federal funds for religious purposes," they wrote.

For their part, the FFRF viewed the settlement as a victory and used their press release announcing the settlement to again criticize the college.

"We have rescued nearly half a million in taxpayers' money," Gaylor said in a statement about the settlement. "Public funds should never have been used to help build a Bible college or indoctrinate a vulnerable set of students. These students deserve true academic remedial aid, not Biblical indoctrination."

However, the FFRF acknowledged that the college could, in their opinion, submit a new action plan, and that the college had received other funds, such as those for counseling services, that were constitutional. However, the FFRF did warn them that they would go back to court if the college were to submit a new action plan.

For college leaders, news of the settlement was frustrating in that Hamilton did not get details of the settlement until he had traveled to Washington, DC to meet with Gaubatz and government officials to find out how the college could legally spend funds. That information would be essential in creating a new action plan.

While in DC in October of 2006, Hamilton and Derek Gaubatz, again from the Becket Fund, led a meeting at the White House Faith-Based and Community Initiatives office, where the staff seemed supportive of the work the college was doing. Staff at the faith-based offices said they'd been in touch with the Departments of Justice and Education, to see what could be done about the college's grants. Then a few days later, it was off to the Department of Education, where they received a letter with the Department's findings that the college had used grant funds for religious purposes—a conclusion that Hamilton disagreed with.

When the meeting ended, Hamilton got a call from the college, saying that a reporter from the *Anchorage Daily News* was seeking comment about the Department of Education's letter, which had been sent to the news media as part of a Freedom From Religion Foundation press release. Leaving the job of replying to the media to Gaubatz, Hamilton turned his efforts toward trying to get a new action spending plan in place to salvage remaining grant funds.

The first step was to spend an afternoon with the U.S. Department of Education liaison at a training session on how the Department of Education funds could be used—training he'd later say would have been helpful to get at the front end of the grant, not the back end. After submitting a series of new spending plans and after months of negotiations, in December of 2006, the college eventually would get approval to use $100,000 of the grant—or about $300,000 less than hoped for but more than the FFRF thought the college should receive. The funds were to be used for academic programs, Gaubatz would tell the Associated Press, when the decision to return some of the funds was announced.

"Part of religious liberty is not discriminating against people of all faiths, of all types," Gaubatz told the AP.

While the legal battles over the Department of Education rolled on, supporters of the college rallied to its aid. By the fall of 2005, a group in Mankato, Minnesota, pledged $30,000 to assist the school. That was followed by $40,000 in pledges from a group in Denver and $40,000 from a group in the Twin Cities. A MIRACLE!

"Many people have ACC close to their hearts and are with us," Hamilton wrote in mid-October 2005, encouraged by the show of support amidst the school's legal woes. "Once again, we will make payroll and are up to date on all bills." A MIRACLE!

Through this entire experience, including Hamilton being interviewed on national Fox News, the reputation of ACC had not been tarnished in any fathomable way through this ordeal, according to Hamilton. Gratefully, the Becket Fund donated all their efforts over the years to ACC, a gift in value exceeding $250,000! The Alliance Defending Freedom also contributed $5,000 toward some of the legal work to be done. No ACC funds were used to pay for any of the attorney costs. A MIRACLE!

During much of this time, life at the college continued to roll on, in large part due to the work of the staff, especially Jeff Siemers, who took on the role of Campus Director in Hamilton's absence. Work on the dining hall also continued in fits and starts—aided in part by a refund of nearly $20,000 from Spenard Builders Supply in Soldotna, where most of the materials for the project had been purchased. A construction loan from National Covenant Properties and a drawdown from reserves also helped move the project forward.

6

The first time Dale Solberg arrived on campus at ACC was in the spring of 2004, and he wondered what he had gotten himself into. The college was off in the woods, with a handful of buildings surrounded by trees, mounds of snow, and darkness. Solberg had been advising Sharon Finifrock on academic library processes and procedures via distance since 2001, but March 2004 was the first time he traveled to Alaska. Solberg had hoped to attend the dedication of the college campus in September of 2001, but his travel plans, like many who had planned to attend the dedication, were disrupted by the 9/11 terrorist attack.

"I thought, oh no," Solberg said, as a passage from the book of Hebrews came to mind. "I'm used to small and remote because I grew up in a small farming town in northeastern North Dakota and I served in public education in a remote and strongly Native American area of western North Dakota, but this was the evidence of things not seen." After serving in western North Dakota in the late 1970s, Solberg had been living and serving in suburban Minneapolis–St. Paul for nearly 25 years.

Solberg had come to Soldotna to see if he could be of help to the then-fledgling college, especially as the school began the process of applying for accreditation, something Solberg had experience with. He had served public schools and Christian day schools and also had experience in Christian higher education.

"As a start-up Christian ministry and college and in a very different context than serving in a suburban and Caucasian setting, ACC seemed the right place. It's certainly been a series of miracles," he said.

He especially knew that accreditation wasn't something that could be rushed, nor just a matter of checking boxes on a form. Instead, it was a long, internal process, that would take years to accomplish, something he tried to make clear in June of 2004 when he was flown from Minnesota to Alaska to take part in a consultative site visit with ABHE staff.

"It's many cycles of overlapping reporting," he said in a May 2024 interview. "It's not just saying you're doing it—it's proving that you're doing it."

The main point he recalled making is that there was no fast track to accreditation. Instead, the staff would work through a long, steady process, which would involve creating the systems and policies that would transform ACC from a start-up to an institution of Christian higher learning. That process—of applying, writing a self-study, going through numerous consultative and evaluative site visits from the accrediting body and from peer reviewers, then moving from Applicant status to Candidate status, and then getting five-year probation Accredited status, and finally initial ten-year Accredited status—would likely take a decade or longer.

"I think people thought that I didn't know what I was talking about," recalled Solberg, a soft-spoken man with a self-deprecating sense of humor and deep love for the college and its students.

Much of the initial work was done by Solberg and Dr. Cheryl Davis, who formed the core of the accreditation team. They wrote the first academic catalog and the first faculty and staff handbooks. They began student advising, tutoring, and academic placement services. They wrote the course descriptions and syllabi guidelines. Solberg's emphases were collecting statistics, working with records management, and compliance issues related to the accreditation process, while Dr. Davis concentrated on academic content, assessment, and planning. Numerous and extensive reports had to be filed with the accrediting body and the U.S. Department of Education. Over the years, Solberg prepared for and hosted eight consultative accreditation site visits and had been part of four evaluative accreditation site visits.

The initial work by Solberg and Davis began a process of assessment and reporting, which eventually led to assembling thousands of pages of the accreditation self-study with three main documents—the Compliance Document, the Assessment Document, and the Planning Document, plus ten appendices. The weight of the shipment of boxes weighed more than 80 pounds because it had to be duplicated five times for the accrediting body and for each peer reviewer, Solberg recalled.

Along the way, the team learned that accreditors shared something in common with the founders of the Evangelical Covenant Church. One of their favorite questions was essentially, "Where is it written?" Behind that question was a reminder of the need to document everything the school did.

"If it's not written down, it didn't happen," Solberg said.

The staff also learned not to fear the process of accreditation and to admit when they didn't know something. Solberg said the process is built on constructive feedback, which only works with complete honesty and transparency, even though the process was somewhat intimidating.

"It's kind of scary, and you want to get it over with and you want to hide things that you don't know," Solberg said. Getting past fear and being open to critique was a crucial step in the process. He recalled that after the first evaluative site visit from ABHE evaluators in 2007, for example, the school was given more than a dozen recommendations for needed changes.

Looking back at accreditation, Solberg says it was key to the college's growth and long-term success. The school was started by youth pastors, who had the ambition and zeal for serving the needs of students, but even the accreditors stressed again and again that ACC must prove that it was an academic institution, he said.

"We started with no students, no money, and no buildings, but with a vision," said Solberg, echoing Hamilton's description of the college's origins. "It was the evidence of things not seen."

Accreditation, he added, gave needed structure to harness the zeal of the college's founders. Solberg's experience and steady, careful approach to his work, as well as the experience that Davis brought to her role, proved an excellent balance to the former youth workers who made up much of the early staff.

Davis would eventually marry Jeff Siemers, one of those former youth pastors that started ACC, and she would go on to become a professor at, and later director of, the Kenai Peninsula College campus not far from ACC.

Being accredited also meant that the college had to find staff who had advanced credentials and experience in higher education, which made the academic programs better. Many of the staff had master's degrees in the areas of expertise ACC needed, but more had to take additional schooling to achieve a master's degree. In order to teach at ACC, each professor in the associate's degree curriculum must have a master's or doctorate degree. ACC would partially support financially those who needed those terminal credentials.

In the first years, all paid staff and faculty were also missionary fundraisers and served multiple administrative staff roles as well as serving as adjunct faculty. Solberg and Davis needed to work very creatively to assign courses to adjunct faculty members. Some courses were designed to be taught in a condensed format of meeting all day for a week or three to four hours in the evening. Qualified adjunct faculty members, both paid and volunteer, some driving quite a distance, were recruited. For some composition courses, Dr. Davis would be the lead teacher and other staff would teach parts of the class based on assessment placement. Two North Park Seminary interns served as faculty members and staff for a full year each. One individual preparing for ordination and preparing to attend seminary, served as a full-time volunteer adjunct faculty member and as registrar for two years. Many of the original faculty and staff members were working on advanced degrees—a first or second master's degree or a doctorate. Solberg managed incoming transcripts for faculty members and kept curriculum vitae and faculty professional development reports current. "The Lord sent the right people at the right time," Solberg said. "I think Keith would testify to that. All processes, but especially writing a massive self-study and preparing for an accreditation site visit wasn't a lone-wolf process. It had to be a group process."

The accreditation process, like much of the college's story, was built on faith. The staff knew there was a job that needed to be done, so they got to work, knowing that with God's help and the help of the right experts, things would work out. And even if they didn't, the school was in God's hands.

"Sometimes I don't know if we knew what the future held," Solberg said in a 2024 interview. "I think many times we thought, if it wasn't for the Holy Spirit, ACC couldn't and wouldn't exist. But it continues, now years later." A MIRACLE!

During the accreditation process, the college also received several grants, which helped the school renovate the library and make other important classroom upgrades. Solberg was also able to reorganize the college's library collection, which includes an extensive collection on the history of the Christian church in Alaska and Alaskan Native culture. The school currently has the second largest theological library in the state, thanks in large part to the donation of books from Alaska Bible College in 2004 and from Sheldon Jackson University in Sitka when it closed in 2007. The physical book collection as of 2025 stands at 16,000 volumes in all collections as well as digital collections numbering in the tens of thousands.

When Alaska Bible College, formerly located in Glennallen and now based in Palmer, shut down its Anchorage campus, the school donated the contents of that campus's library, about 5,000 books, to Alaska Christian College. Alan and Sharon Finifrock, who were tasked with moving the books to campus, loaded up a pair of vans with as many boxes as they could and made the three-hour drive up Alaska Highway 1 to Anchorage to get them.

"We had gathered banana boxes, apple boxes and orange boxes from the local stores, and we filled the back of our vans with those boxes and drove up there," she said. "I think we spent two days, possibly part of a third day, going through those books. Of course, being a booklover and having worked in libraries and so forth, Al teased me by saying the problem was Sharon thought we had to read every book before we came back."

As they were taking the books off the shelves at the Bible college, the Finifrocks used a technique they'd learned from Northwestern College in Minneapolis, when that school moved its library. As they took books off the shelf, they put them in boxes in order, based on the Dewey Decimal System number on each book. Then they put a card on the outside of the box to note which numbers were inside.

When they got back to the school, with more than 50 boxes of books, they were all stored in the rec room, which by that point was no longer used to house students, until the school's maintenance staff could arrange shelving for all the books. The wooden covering over the pool, built by Bob Bode, became the new flooring for the growing library collection.

The Finifrocks started the process of getting the library in order, with the help of some volunteers.

"We also got the card catalog from Alaska Bible College, and so we did have some record of what we had," she said. "But for some reason, we didn't have a card on file for every book. So some of the volunteers were typing out card catalog cards."

Around this time, Solberg arrived on campus and created an electronic card catalog system for all the books in the library. By then, the collection had grown to about 7,000 volumes. Solberg oversaw the conversion to a digital format and Sharon Finifrock had dozens of volumes barcoded, re-labeled, and placed call number labels on each book. The project took about a year and a half.

Initially, Solberg recalled being perplexed at how long it took some of the students to get their work done or to respond to questions in class. Then Davis reminded him that many of the students were bilingual learners, having been taught in the early grades in Yup'ik, a Native language—so they were thinking in Yup'ik and then translating on the fly into English, not an easy task and one that students who grew up speaking and learning in English did not have to do.

He also learned, little by little, about some of the challenges students had faced growing up. Some of the most profound times in those early years, he said, came when classes were put on hold for a week for a visit by Clair and Clara Schnupp, a Mennonite couple from Ontario, Canada, who had extensive experience in counseling ministry. The whole week would be set aside for group meetings with the Schnupps, with individual counseling for students—in a precursor of what the ministry of New Hope Counseling Center would become. Solberg said he was also struck at how this older Canadian couple had a way of connecting with students and helped them make progress in dealing with some of the hurts from their past. The Schnupps were respected as elders by the students.

Solberg said that he also learned to have patience with students. Solberg said he'd grown up in a very strict environment with clear rules about right and wrong and sometimes had trouble understanding why college students sometimes got into trouble or struggled with alcohol and other issues. Compounding things, in the early years, many of the students lived and went to class in the same building—

meaning there was little space to hide when things went wrong and lots of potential for conflicts and misunderstandings.

"It wasn't always one big happy family," he said.

Then there were other challenges. Many of the other students had grown up in tight-knit small villages off the road system, so moving to Soldotna, a community of about 5,000 on the road system, could bring with it some culture shock. Solberg recalled teaching one of the students, who had never been behind the wheel of a car, how to drive, and being surprised at how intimidating the road system could be. Also, he could empathize with how difficult it could be to be away from home and in a new tight-knit community for the students.

By 2008, the college received the news that ACC had been granted Candidate status for accreditation, a major move toward fully accredited status, but with many of the benefits of accredited status. That first milestone had been awaited with bated breath. A MIRACLE! That moment brought back memories of the long struggle that the staff had been through. After submitting about 1,000 pages of documentation and undergoing a site visit, the staff was worn out.

"I mean, there were red marks on every page," he recalled. "And then very clear recommendations, which were actually requirements. And, we had only six weeks to respond."

Then it was off to meet with the Commission on Accreditation that would decide the fate of the college's results of their efforts. The college had a good idea that their efforts would be approved. Otherwise, why call them to a meeting about the accreditation? Still, there was tension.

"I remember going into that room," he said. "We didn't know what the questions would be. And while they were colleagues, they looked stern. It was a little tense, but it was celebratory as well."

Jeff Siemers said that accreditation played an underappreciated role in the history of ACC. In the early years, he said, the college had no way of measuring the effectiveness of its programs, aside from counting how many students stayed for the year or how many graduated. But the school wasn't keeping transcripts, because, for the most part, students who graduated weren't trying to transfer those credits to other schools. The school didn't have a system for grading work or evaluating student progress, and couldn't show prospective students or their parents the value of coming to ACC in any quantifiable way.

Siemers and other leaders were also becoming aware that they had to show that coming to the school had measurable value. Otherwise, few families could afford to spend $10-12,000 a year to send their students to ACC for the spiritual and social benefit alone—even though that part of the school's program was essential. The lawsuit over the Department of Education grants also showed that outsiders would be keeping a close eye on what the college was doing, and becoming accredited would help validate the college's mission and programs.

Jeff Siemers said that the work done by Solberg and Cheryl Davis on accreditation helped bring legitimacy to the academic programs of the school. It also helped the college understand where things were going well and where they weren't—and what was needed to succeed in higher education.

"We didn't know the answers—because we didn't know the questions," Siemers said in a May 2024 interview at a coffee shop not far from the college campus. At the time, Siemers, who had just finished his doctorate at the Institute for Doctoral Studies in the Visual Arts and was the college's executive vice president, was taking a quick break between preparations for graduation the following day.

He gave credit to Dr. Chuck Faber, the longtime Dean at Boise Bible College, who led a team assessing the programs at ACC for the ABHE, for helping the college understand the link between its mission of preparing young people for whole-life discipleship and the broader academic world. That mission, while important, didn't have any academic meaning or tell students or outsiders what the college did to help students learn or what they would learn on campus.

Faber also helped ACC's leaders think through what success would be like for their students—because knowing what the goal was would help shape how the college ran its programs. Faber pointed to his institution as an example.

"I remember Dr. Faber coming and saying, 'Look, if we don't, if 100 percent of our graduates don't go into the pastorate after they graduate from BBC, we feel like it's a failure,'" Siemers said. "He was that direct and blunt."

ACC would have different goals but needed that kind of focus, Siemers and other ACC leaders learned. Accreditation also provided a "rubric for sustainability," helping the college think through every part of its program, from the campus physical plant and finances to the grading system and academic requirements for the faculty.

"You learn so much about being an institution," he said. "So many places could go through that and be able to benefit from it."

For Hamilton, the accreditation process meant revising the college's strategic plan and working on addressing some of the major weaknesses in the college's programs that the self-evaluation process had revealed—as well as trying to raise an additional $25,000 to complete the dining hall project.

By the end of 2006, the college had received some much-needed infusions of cash, including $28,000 raised during a fifth-anniversary dinner, along with nearly $50,000 in future donations pledged to the school. Hamilton also received word that the college had been named as beneficiary for a charitable trust valued at close to $200,000—which would be given to the college as a bequest in the future.

All of that was a relief, as Hamilton hoped to leave for his first sabbatical in early January, knowing that little money would be raised during the time he was gone.

The year ended with a pair of weddings, where both couples, Buzz Cree and Charelle Geffe and Adam London and Shirleen Wong, were alums of ACC, along with hopes that the dining hall would finally be completed in time for their weddings. Just before Christmas, the college community gathered for an end-of-year service of candles and community celebration in the nearly completed facility.

> I remember talking to Keith, my youth pastor at Arvada Covenant, in between church services and asking him how the forming of ACC was coming along. He said they didn't have many staff yet, were still looking for a location, didn't have much money, and still needed students. I left that pew thinking Keith was crazy. But by the time I had reached the sanctuary doors, God had convinced me that I should attend ACC. As a student during the first year, none of us knew what to expect, but we all had a sense that God had called us to ACC for a reason.
>
> Two things completely changed my life that first year of ACC: reading through the entire Bible, cover to cover, and going through Biblical counseling to forgive my abusive father.
>
> —Adam London

"It was a glorious service with great acoustics and singing, and the new fireplace was magnificent," Hamilton wrote in his journal. "I am excited to see it all upon my return from my sabbatical when it will all be completed."

Hamilton returned that May after several months, just in time for the dedication of the new Peninsula Conference Center, as the dining hall facility was named, and to attend graduation services for seven first-year students as well as five second-year students who completed their associate's degrees.

He recalled one student who had been dismissed just before leaving for his sabbatical. The student had sent a letter begging to be able to return, was going to go get counseling, and was basically homeless. Hamilton's last act before disappearing on sabbatical was to approve this student's re-entry, not believing it would likely end up any different than the last semester's results. Upon return in May, at the end-of-the-year retreat, Hamilton looked all over the crowd gathered at dinner for this specific student. He wasn't to be found anywhere in the worship center at the camp. With sadness, Hamilton asked Curtis Ivanoff what happened to that student who obviously didn't complete the spring semester, likely being released. Curtis said, "What do you mean, he's right there coming out of the bathroom now!" Hamilton hugged that student and said to him directly, eye to eye, "Of all the students I was hoping to see after my four months gone, you were number one." That student did graduate from ACC and lives locally with his family.

Many lives of students continued to be impacted. One of the students during this period that made a name for Alaska, Katherine Rae Fancher, an ACC graduate, became the first Alaska Native woman to attend the U.S. Naval Academy. Fancher, who'd grown up in Unalakleet, attended ACC in 2006 after graduation from high school, before making her way to the Naval Academy campus in Annapolis, Maryland.

Her time at ACC had been life changing. As a young girl, Fancher had been hurt, which left her feeling numb and hopeless for much of her childhood—so much so that she considered taking her own life. During her time at ACC, she'd been able to open up about her past, and, with the help of counselors and supportive staff, had been able to experience healing from the shame and hurt she'd experienced.

Still, she struggled during her first year at the Academy to adjust to the dual culture shocks of life outside of Alaska and the demands of military life. Her grades suffered and she wondered if she'd made a mistake.

"Up until that point, it was me knowing that this is where God has brought me, this is where Christ has led me, so I'm going to stay the path as much as I hated it," she later told a reporter for the Evangelical Covenant Church, her home denomination. "Second semester, senior year, I was like, 'You know what, I like this, I enjoy this.'"

Fancher's success was a reminder of what was possible for students who attended ACC.

With the dining hall completed, Hamilton turned his eyes to a new project—the purchase of a log cabin and five acres adjacent to the college. The building, which cost $130,000, could serve as staff housing during the school year and be rented out in the summer to provide additional income from the school. Along with donations and tuition, Hamilton had begun to look for additional streams of revenue, including using the campus to host conferences as well as tourists during the summer fishing season. Eventually the cabin would be sold and relocated to make room for the construction of the New Hope Counseling Center, ideally, in close proximity to the campus.

Buying the cabin was a leap of faith, as the building needed about $20,000 in repairs. ACC still found itself cash-strapped in the wake of the lawsuit over the Department of Education grants, and while it was a great opportunity, it was one that currently ACC could ill-afford.

Still, there were signs that the college should move forward with the purchase. LeRoy Lundell, from Minnetonka, Minnesota, a longtime supporter, gave a donation of $25,000 toward the purchase of the cabin, while the Ideker Family Foundation gave another $15,000 to cover costs leftover from the dining hall. Not long afterward, following a service at Redeemer Covenant Church, Brooklyn Park, Minnesota, another $40,000 gift arrived unexpectedly after Hamilton had been there on the "potluck trail." A MIRACLE!

By the end of the summer, the purchase of the new/old log cabin between campus and Poppy Lane Flowers was complete, just in time for staff to move in and rent the cabin ahead of the beginning of the school year.

In mid-February 2008, the Hamiltons, Siemers, and Solbergs—along with Krista and Rev. Scott Pitsch, another long-term staff couple—made their way to Orlando for a meeting with the ABHE Commission on Accreditation that was evaluating their status for accreditation. If they were granted Candidate status, it would be a major step forward and the start of a three-year process toward probationary accreditation. It would also open the door for students to receive federal financial aid through the FAFSA and Pell Grant/Student Loan programs.

"Lord, you know the plans for ACC and our students/staff," Hamilton wrote in his journal on the eve of the ABHE meeting. "You have provided since day one the miracles of this place. We humbly ask for your favor in this matter. Our trust is in you."

On February 20, after a hectic night of travel that was nearly derailed by flight delays out of the Kenai airport, Hamilton arrived in Florida at 7:45 in the morning, leaving just enough time for him to shower and change before running to the Orlando hotel where the meeting with the ABHE Commission on Accreditation was being held. After a summary of the programs at ACC, along with re-telling the amazing story of Rae Fancher's experience, the ACC alum–turned–Naval Academy graduate, the ACC staff faced a series of questions from the Commission, which they answered with relative ease.

The ACC staffers, who had expected to wait a few days for a decision, were then asked to leave the room while the Commission deliberated about their status. A few minutes later, they were called back into the room, when they learned their Candidate status was approved.

"We sat in silence thinking there was more, then they said, 'That's all!'" Hamilton recounted in his journals. "We were amazed. So quick and it was over. Five years of work, waiting, and suspense was over. We were Candidates! They all stood and clapped for us, shook our hands, and a few hugs ensued. We walked out, stunned and grateful." A MIRACLE!

7

After celebrating the news that the college had taken the first major step toward accreditation, the staff took a day to celebrate and catch their breath. Then it was back to work, especially for Krista Pitsch, the college's director of financial aid, who was tasked with getting the college ready for students to use the Free Application for Federal Student Aid, better known as the FAFSA form. Colleges around the country use this application to determine how much financial aid students are eligible to receive, heavily based on their parents' capacity to pay for the cost of the education. In the case of the typical ACC student, over 90 percent of families are unable to pay anything toward their student's education.

ACC's access to FASFA meant the college could charge more for tuition and room and board, from about $10,000 to $13,000, a much-needed increase as ACC was always undervalued in charging the actual cost. Even more importantly, it meant that students would have access to financial assistance to pay their bills.

This had become an ongoing concern for most of the college's existence. Many students lacked the financial resources to pay even the modest cost of attending ACC, leaving the college in the position of either forgiving their debt or pressuring students to pay their bills through loans, which ultimately proved to be counterproductive.

"This would be an incredible blessing, to not only charge $3,000 more, but to actually collect most all of it from students," Hamilton wrote in his journals about what access to financial aid might mean for students and the college. He estimated that the access to aid might bring as much as $300,000 a year in additional revenue for the college—a boon as the school struggled to keep up with operating expenses such as payroll, which remained a constant struggle.

While on a fundraising trip that spring to Minnesota and Seattle, the Lord provided about $41,500 in donations. However, the college needed $40,000 to pay payroll and other expenses, meaning funds were still going out just as fast as they came in. As a result of the continued tight finances, the college's board decided to freeze any new construction projects for three years—meaning that the New Hope Counseling Center, rather than having a new building of its own, would move into the right side of the duplex the college had built.

"We are all concerned about the budget, the employee pensions being paid in full, the triplex apartment purchase which was an option for us, and future steps with accreditation," Hamilton recalled in his journals. The college was also in the midst of turnover, needing to hire a director of admissions, assistant director of development, two female resident assistants, and an academic dean—all at the same time. Harvey and Linda Lundquist, a couple from Turlock, California, had also joined the staff to oversee facilities and human resources—and became long-term members of the college staff. Harvey recently retired in October of 2024 after 17 years and continues to volunteer on the campus in maintenance.

By early May of 2008, another year had passed and it was time for graduation. Forty-two students had started the previous fall, with 27 making it to the end of the semester. Of those 27, 11 would graduate between the first- and second-year programs. There was a silver lining in those numbers. On the surface, it was the worst attrition rate in the college's history, with a third of the students having failed to complete the year.

"However, this class this semester was all committed to all being here in every way and the 27 were a mighty bunch of disciples," Hamilton would recount in his journals, noting that nine of the students had been baptized just before graduation. The graduation ceremony also packed out nearby Peninsula Grace Church, a great sign of support for the students by their friends and family.

Adam London was named Alumnus of the Year, while Stephanie Olrun and Lupi Anaver were named Students of the Year. Many of the students were expected back in the fall as the college's second-year program continued to grow.

After a trip south to California for fundraising and then a conference put on by the Murdock Trust in Washington, followed by some family time on vacation, Hamilton returned to campus in June to find summer volunteers for Forest Park Covenant Church in Michigan hard at work. During a break from work, one of the team members from Forest Park struck up a conversation with Hamilton at the local Short Stop Grocery where Hamilton was buying a round of ice cream. He asked how the buildings on campus got their names. Most, said Hamilton, were named for the churches who built them and provided some funding for them. That led to a question: What was the next big project needed for the school?

For Hamilton, there were two big answers. The New Hope Counseling Center needed a new home. They had quickly outgrown the right side of the duplex apartment building as they had recently opened up counseling to the broader Kenai Peninsula community. The school also needed a major donor to help complete or make a down payment on the purchase of that nearby triplex, a seven bedroom apartment building that would serve as staff housing as well as provide a source of rental income during the tourist season. Hamilton asked Roger Eikenberry if he and his wife, Jan, would consider a $150,000 gift for the counseling center construction. Within seconds, he said, "I can do that." What? A 32-second conversation with that amazing response? A MIRACLE! When Hamilton got home, he told his wife Debbie about the conversation. He told her he felt that man was pulling his leg. Debbie told Keith to go and find out! Hamilton was perplexed. He really needed to ask this couple for the $150,000 gift toward the triplex, not NHCC. So, partway through the week, Hamilton suggested instead a major down payment towards the $280,000 final asking price.

On Saturday, as the couple was leaving with their team to head back to Michigan, a follow-up conversation ensued with Hamilton in his office. They first said to Hamilton, "We've noticed there is a lot of equipment around the campus for recreation items that need a home. We'd like to give you funding to build a sports shack. Hamilton figured that would be around $15,000, one-tenth of the request he had made a few days earlier. Rats! But that wasn't all. They also committed the $150,000 to purchase the triplex! Hamilton was ecstatic. Then, another final commitment came from this couple that had just sold their grocery stores and were desiring to give a gift to ministry. They committed the first $75,000 toward building the counseling center! Leaders from Forest Park Covenant Church pledged the other matching $75,000 needed to finish the counseling center. By August, Forest Park had plans for the new counseling center underway, with a commitment to return the following summer to frame the center over a two-week period. Again, Richard Borgeson, their architect, stepped up to complete the plans for NHCC. That one purchase of two dollars for ice cream at the store became a final gift of $315,000 to ACC for building NHCC on the property of the old log cabin adjacent to campus, and the purchase of a much-needed apartment building also adjacent to campus. Of course, the sports shack was amazing too. Roger Eikenberry was able to see all three building projects completed before he passed. So, who would next like to have ice cream with Dr. Hamilton? A MIRACLE!

During an interview in May of 2024, Debbie Hamilton said she was grateful for the generosity of the many volunteers and supporters, like those from Forest Park, who helped make the ministry of the counseling center, and the college as a whole, possible. Today, the name Forest Park is proudly placed at the front door of the center, along with the duplex having the names of the North Mankato and Iron Mountain Covenant Churches for their role in providing funds for and building these structures.

Debbie Hamilton said that the counseling center and college were built on the faithful prayers and support of volunteers who saw the need the school was trying to meet and decided to help out. That kind of expansive approach to ministry has been key to the school's survival and ability to thrive. The school was not built on the vision or genius of just one person. Instead, a number of people showed up at the right place at the right time, with the right skills and experience—and especially the willingness to stand up and help even when the way forward seemed unclear, and give generous gifts.

Building ACC needed to be done—and so people came and built it. And they did so because of a love for the students who attend the school, said Debbie Hamilton.

"Part of it is that we're all parents at heart," she said. "Our hearts are so moved by these young students, and we hear their stories. Every fiber in your being just wants to love on them and help them be successful."

As the counseling center grew, the staff there began to expand the services the center provided. Along with therapy and help with issues like depression, grief, and substance abuse—something that many Alaska young people, especially those from Native communities, deal with—counselors also began helping students heal from the trauma they had experienced.

The center has also worked hard to help students overcome some of the stigma of seeking help for mental health issues, for both students and, later on, for community residents. The idea has been to help people understand that counseling can be a proactive way to address some of the struggles of life, rather than an indicator of something for people who are struggling. Going to counseling is not a sign of failure, Debbie Hamilton said. Instead, it can be a positive choice for self-care.

"The reality is that life is hard for everyone and everybody has a story," Debbie Hamilton said. "Counseling is an opportunity to go explore your story, and to gain some tools and some resources to be able to address any pain that might be in your story."

Debbie Hamilton said that sometimes students—as well as other clients the counseling center sees—need another set of eyes to help them look at their situation and find a way forward. She said that students have often come to the school having family and friends, but haven't had the support or resources to deal with the grief from home. So, they try to make do the best that they can and can suffer in silence, not knowing that other people struggle as well and can help them deal with grief and loss.

"Sometimes we just don't know any other way," she said.

Debbie Hamilton said that many Alaskans are still dealing with the changes that the last century brought, from the influenza and other illnesses that hit the state in the early 1900s to the rapid Westernization that statehood brought, where so much of the communal way of life that had sustained Native communities was lost. She pointed in particular to the writing of Velma Wallis, an Alaska writer of Gwich'in descent, who grew up in the remote community of Fort Yukon. She detailed many of the challenges Native communities faced in her 2003 book, *Raising Ourselves*.

In their work, Debbie Hamilton and other counselors try to combine spiritual support and nurture with some of the latest trauma intervention strategies as they help students navigate their past challenges and prepare for the future. It's a complicated task, she admitted, one that involves building trust over time. That's one reason that the college does not require that students go to counseling unless it is part of a recovery plan from discipline issues. Instead, the staff tries to build a safe and supportive environment that makes seeking help in counseling possible.

She said that in the early years of Alaska Christian College, the staff relied heavily on the approach used by Covenant Bible College. That was helpful in designing many of the courses and the behind-the-scenes structures needed to run a college. But CBC and Alaska Christian College weren't dealing with the same population of students. Students who went to CBC often came from intact church families and were used to a more Western model of education—and as a result, had fewer academic challenges or past trauma to deal with.

Both schools were helping students deal with the challenges of being away from home and learning to make decisions on their own. And, like many young people away from home for the first time, students at both schools made mistakes and needed guidance along the way. But to be successful, Alaska Christian College needed to find a model that would work for students in its own context, not someone else's.

Hamilton said that the government funds the school received for counseling services and the support from churches like Forest Park were game changers for the college, allowing the college to have the kind of intensive support service that students need.

"We've really encouraged students to be proactive and not wait for a crisis," she said.

Despite the much-needed support for the counseling center, finances remained tight and by August of 2008, the college was once again struggling to make payroll. The college's financial challenges were exacerbated that fall when a smaller-than-expected class arrived on campus and 2008 was the first year all second-year courses had to be offered on campus at ACC, not through the partnership with KPC. This meant more faculty members were needed, and more of everything, thus more finances were also needed. That combined with the college's commitment to accepting students, regardless of their ability to pay, made it difficult to make ends meet. ACC has always been a mission college, allowing students for their first year to come and join the college with the expectation that funding will come in from various sources. No student has been denied enrollment at ACC their first semester based on ability to pay. The Lord has taken care of ACC these 25 years with that missional commitment in mind.

"We again are under expectations for budgeted needs, yet, we find ourselves in the full desire to serve these that are here versus the ones we know that should also be here joining them," Keith Hamilton wrote in his journal as the fall semester began.

Yet, support for the college overall remained adequate. An unexpected $20,000 gift was followed by news that the Murdock Trust would award the college a $110,000 grant for the counseling center to add to the $150,000 from Forest Park. A MIRACLE! That grant meant that New Hope Counseling Center was fully funded! In addition, the college closed on the triplex apartment adjacent to the campus, giving the school an added source of rental income. For the triplex, the fund was still $20,000 short needed to pay the seller in full. When the seller heard how close they were, he tithed back 10 percent, thus paying for it in full with his own money! A MIRACLE! That was then followed by a $25,000 gift that allowed the college to make payroll once again.

Delays in getting the college qualified for other funding sources, such as Pell Grants and Title III funding for Indigenous students, along with Title IV funds for financial aid, put pressure on the staff to raise funds for their salaries, on top of their workload at the school. Keith Hamilton summed up the college's financial situation this way in his journal, early in 2008: "It is all a maze of pieces; so much blessing for building and wish list items, but not enough operational funding."

In October, the good news arrived that the Department of Education had approved ACC to receive Title IV financial aid and that students would be able to use FAFSA funding. However, that was tempered by a stock market crash in the fall of 2008. On October 8, the Dow Jones Industrial Average dropped by 679 points—the third-largest daily drop in its history. *The Washington Post* reported it was the first time in five years the Dow had dropped by 9,000. The October 8 plunge was part of the ongoing decline in the stock market, which had peaked above 14,000 the prior year. Not long after the historic fall, a major donor called with bad news, because of the stock market, they would not be able to make planned end-of-the-year gifts. With the majority of ACC's budget reliant on donations, a prolonged downturn was worrisome.

There was some good news. A fundraising dinner for the counseling center brought in $11,000 in gifts, while in late November, Keith Hamilton learned that ChangePoint Alaska, an Anchorage-based megachurch, would devote its annual Christmas offering to the college. ChangePoint also invited Hamilton to speak at services in early December, followed by several students giving their testimonies later in the month. All told, ChangePoint would donate $111,000 to the college to pay off *all* students carrying any college debt! Not one student owed ACC that entire year. A MIRACLE! Most of that gift would be put into savings after paying down the student accounts as part of a rainy-day fund for dealing with the fallout from the nation's financial crisis.

Twenty-seven students returned to campus to start the new academic year in 2009, still below capacity—with the staff well aware of the need to grow enrollment, especially given that a recession was likely, which could lead to fewer donations. The staff also began making preemptive cuts in the budget, knowing the importance of cutting costs. By spring break, all the school's bills were paid, without touching the $100,000 rainy-day fund, with an additional $35,000 from FAFSA funds still unspent as well. Hamilton also began taking on a few 12- or 24-hour shifts at the local fire department to help complement his ACC salary.

Planning for the 2010 fiscal year meant more cuts, with most of the staff being put on 10- or 11-month contracts for the school year, rather than being paid for the entire calendar year to reduce costs. The need for more revenue also meant that for the first time, students would be able to take out federal loans to pay for their education at ACC, a decision that college leaders made with some trepidation as the loans came with risk for both students and the school. Not only might students take on debt, but if they could not repay the loans, then other federal funds for the college might be jeopardized.

"We are at risk either way," Hamilton wrote in his journal that spring. "I will again trust God that this is the best course for us." He went on to recount that the school year ended with more worries about finances. While the college was able to make payroll in April, the outlook for May was "bleak," as giving was down by $60,000 for the year.

The students, however, seemed to be thriving, with 10 first-year and two second-year students graduating, and 14 students, or 60 percent of the class, hoping to return that fall. "God always reminded us that He was the Provider and that our students were worth all the work and effort to give them their best opportunity for Christian higher education," Hamilton later wrote in his journal.

By the time Hamilton had returned from the denominational Covenant Annual meeting, about 30 volunteers from Muskegon, Michigan, were on campus, hard at work on raising the new counseling center and completing the framing, siding, and roofing within the first few weeks. That was followed by sheet rocking, with a professional drywall finisher set to arrive on campus to tape the walls and get them ready for painting.

August was filled with Hamilton making plans for fundraising during his downtimes at the local fire station, where he spent the month of August on unpaid leave from the college to save funds. That included making plans for the annual fundraising dinner—an event that became even more crucial as word trickled in that some of the school's major donors would not be able to give that year because of the recession.

In September, the school made payroll with the help of a $10,000 gift as well as the influx of FAFSA funds, which offset some of the decline in giving. A boost in enrollment, including a student from Russia and another from Oman who had been in the U.S. for quite awhile, meant that 40 students were on campus that fall—up from only 30 students the previous year. Good news!

In January, there was more good news, thanks to the effort of the college enrollment staff led by Curtis Ivanoff. The student body had grown to 44, the highest total in the college's history. Some were older students who had returned to take classes at Kenai Peninsula College, while others were siblings or cousins of current students. Almost all the students, 42 in all, made it through to graduation weekend, which again was cause for celebration.

The fall of 2010 brought news that the school had received a five-year, $2.8 million Title III Native-serving federal grant to remodel the library, install a computer lab, and build two additional classrooms as part of a new, million-dollar student success center, along with salaries, which would have been a huge boon for the college. By the spring of 2011, news came that Title III funding had been cut from the federal budget due to the ongoing recession—meaning at least a temporary halt to the construction of the new student center until the ramifications of the cuts in funding had been sorted out.

Eventually, the school learned that, with the help of U.S. Representative Young and U.S. Senator Murkowski, most of the funding for one year of the grant was restored, though any future funding was uncertain. Eventually, the college's Board of Trustees, with guidance from the President's Advisory Council (PAC), would go ahead with the student success center project, in hopes that the government funding would come through in the end, with a groundbreaking for the project held in late April, just before the college's graduation. In the meantime, the college would end up with about $575,000 in loan debt once the project was completed.

"This is another faith test for our team, our trustees, and the PAC, who have also been involved," Hamilton would later recount in his journals. "With a little trembling, we move forward with expectancy."

Graduation that year meant a farewell not just to the students but also to the Finifrocks and to Curtis and Kristi Ivanoff, as earlier that spring, Curtis had been nominated to serve as field director of the Covenant's work in Alaska. It was a bittersweet parting for Ivanoff, who returned to the college in 2008 after taking a year away to earn a master's degree at North Park Theological Seminary in Chicago.

Leaving was difficult, Ivanoff said in a 2024 interview. He loved working with college students and knew the importance of campus ministry, something he'd experienced as a student himself in Oklahoma, where he'd taken an active role at a Baptist student ministry and something he'd seen again and again among the students he taught at ACC.

"It can be a real foundational and trajectory setting for your life," said Ivanoff.

Along with seeing the spiritual growth of students, one of the highlights of Ivanoff's time at the college was his experience teaching the history of Christianity in Alaska, especially among Alaska Natives. It was a course that grew out of his time at North Park Seminary. Ivanoff had already been a fan of history before seminary, a love that grew during his studies in Chicago. The more he read about church history, especially the Covenant's history in Alaska during his time in seminary, the more that history came to life. His interest in the Alaska Covenant had a personal connection—his great-grandfather, Stephan Ivanoff, was one of the first converts in the Covenant church in Alaska and he became a translator for early missionaries in the 1880s.

Like all history, he said, the story of Christianity in Alaska is complicated.

"It's also fraught with some pain because there's complexities," he said. "But it is an amazing story."

Through the class, Ivanoff wanted his students to understand their own stories and the decisions that shaped the church in Alaska. Among those decisions was the "Comity Plan," an agreement negotiated by famed Presbyterian missionary Sheldon Jackson to divide the state by religion, with different denominations—Baptists, Moravians, Presbyterians, Covenanters, Quakers, and Episcopalians among them. That shaped how Alaskan Christians experienced their faith. The Covenant Church was assigned to western Alaska.

Students learned about Protestant missionaries but also of Orthodox priests who brought the faith across the Bering Sea from Russia. (Alaska had been a Russian territory before it became part of the United States in the 1860s.) Alaska became one of the places where the Eastern Church and Western Church met up as the gospel spread around the globe, said Ivanoff. Some of the students came from regions where those two traditions met.

"I find it helpful to understand that it is not a one-size-fits-all story," he said. During class discussions, students would learn about the regions of the state they came from and begin to connect their own stories to the larger history of the church in Alaska. He would also invite them to explore the history of the churches and villages they had grown up in to see a larger story.

He said that maritime peoples, like those in Alaska, navigated by stars, often looking backward in order to find out where they were going. Remembering their history could help students recall that lesson, which is sometimes lost in Western culture, with its constant focus on the future. There were students in almost every class he taught that found a family member mentioned as a part of the church historical record in Alaska.

"There's not time (to look back)," he said during a 2024 interview, reflecting on what Alaska Native Christians had to teach the broader church. "I think it weakens us. It's dangerous not to remember."

Graduation in May was followed by the 10th year reunion, with about 50 former students and staff, what Hamilton would refer to as an "army of disciples," gathered over four days of worship, baseball, and conversation over meals. Kim Kakakaway, who had been named Alumna of the Year, spoke, as did Hamilton, Ivanoff, and Paul Wilson, who had traveled from California to be part of the celebration.

During that summer, the college staff began work on a project that would take more than 15 years to come to fruition—an on-campus, indoor gymnasium/athletic center where students could play basketball and have a place to gather and exercise during the long winter months. That kind of recreation could offer a healthy alternative to long hours spent inside during the winter, and a place where students could walk to on campus. The hope was that an athletic center would also draw students to campus and aid in retention.

"Praying," Hamilton first wrote in his journal in 2002, ahead of a planned board meeting to talk about the feasibility of an athletic center project. It was a prophetic word in some ways—as Hamilton and other leaders would spend more than two decades praying that the gym would move from dream to funding to reality.

That summer was filled with maintenance work—led by longtime volunteers Dick Nelson (Rockford, Illinois), Jim Ramsey (Arvada, Colorado), and Glen Mehrkens (Red Wing, Minnesota), all of whom had played key roles in constructing the largest buildings on campus. They were involved in the building of the Quyana Residence Hall and the Peninsula Conference Center dining building, two of three phases of the master plan to house and feed up to 75 students. They were returning to help maintain the school's growing number of buildings. They were known as the "A-Team" on campus. Each one was rewarded at the beginning of their summer of work with their own large tub of favorite ice cream from Short Stop as payment.

"Our new buildings are now becoming old buildings, needing repairs," Hamilton wrote that summer about the need for ongoing maintenance. While volunteers were busy painting, laying new floors, and taking care of another key project, like renovating the school's library, the new student success center (classroom) building was coming together, built by professional contractors paid for by the Title III grant. By July, that building was roofed and weathered in, with hopes for a completion in the fall, ahead of another accreditation visit by the Association for Biblical Higher Education team.

The summer ended with news that the college had been granted a $180,000 grant from the Murdock Foundation, again, this time to fund a new Director of Development position for the college, as well as the news that Jeremy Rupp from Minnesota had agreed to be the school's Director of Enrollment, meaning that the college was on the road to being fully staffed in time to greet the 40 students arriving that fall. Rupp's parents, Jay and Sandy Rupp, also joined them and led the spiritual life needs for the coming year. They continue to serve annually at ACC as Pastors in Residence.

"God is faithful to be our Provider," Hamilton wrote as the school year began. "He is our Lord of all."

8

A decade into its history, Alaska Christian College remained dependent on miracles to keep its doors open, and often, just when things were going well, another challenge arose. That was the case in the fall of 2011, which had begun with promise after news of the Murdock Trust grant being funded.

Forty-seven students had arrived that fall, a solid class and large enough that the school's finances seemed on solid ground. However, many of the students who arrived that fall were especially troubled and struggled with alcohol in a way that past students had not. By October, 11 of the 47 students had left campus due to multiple violations. Along with the heartache of losing so many students, the college was also forced to make about $70,000 in budget cuts, which included laying off staff, with fears of more cuts on the horizon.

The college had also borrowed $100,000 from National Covenant Properties through its line of credit, a loan that was soon coming due, a reality that sent Hamilton back out on the road to raise funds. Those fiscal woes came right about the time of the final site visit for accreditation, another turning point moment for the college, with a key report due that November.

More bad news followed that fall, and by Thanksgiving, enrollment was down to 30 students. A bad snowstorm drove down attendance at the college's annual fundraising dinner, which brought in only about $30,000, much less than the college needed.

"We are in great financial need, Lord," Hamilton would later write in his journals, recounting the college's financial need. "You own the caribou on a thousand hills.... Help us, O Lord, big time. In Jesus' name, amen."

Things began to turn around after the new year, with 49 students on campus, due in large part to the efforts of the enrollment staff, with hopes that most of the students would make it through the end of the school year. In February 2012, the college received news from AHBE that its accreditation (five-year probationary) had been approved—another step forward and A MIRACLE!

Although 42 students made it to the end of the year, many struggled, despite the new support systems the college had in place, including a new classroom building for student support. Three second-year students graduated, all of them part of the second-year program. None of the first-year students graduated, a disappointment to the staff, but not unexpected given the struggles of the past year.

Cash flow also remained an ongoing concern for the college, which was unable to make payroll, and a troubling sign with the summer approaching. A bequest of about $63,500 from the estate of Marjorie Ruden, a longtime supporter from Arvada, Colorado, surely helped, as did a small grant from the Murdock Trust.

The cash flow issues again turned the spotlight on the dilemma that college leaders faced in trying to build a sustainable institution. Namely, that it proved easier to raise money for capital projects, like a new residence hall and student services building, than to raise funds for ongoing expenses, like paying staff salaries and keeping the lights on. The students that ACC served came in with many needs, often requiring counseling and academic remediation, yet had few finances to draw on to pay for the program that could help them overcome those needs.

Although the college had a track record of building a caring and loving Christian community, helping students thrive was no simple task, and one that got increasingly difficult over the years, as the experiences of ACC's students and their struggles with mental health foreshadowed the kinds of challenges many of their peers around the country would experience over the next two decades. The systems in place for students, especially educational loans, were also built on the assumption that those students would graduate into careers that would allow them to then repay the money they'd borrowed, assumptions that for many students at ACC and other institutions were no longer valid.

The college was also still a work-in-progress after more than a decade of ministry, with the need to grow its donor base, find the right mix of staff and faculty, attract new leaders to replace those who had moved on from the early days, and develop the kind of facilities needed to grow the school. For example, the college could not grow its student population to a sustainable level if there was no place to house them, meaning that another residence hall on campus was needed. Then there was the long-term hope of building an athletic center on campus as well as a new access road onto campus.

Then there was the reality that as a start-up college with a niche audience and mission with precarious finances, ACC had to find people who were comfortable with risk and willing to go out and raise the kind of outside support needed to fund their salaries in many cases, or to find retirees or older volunteers who would give themselves to the school's mission.

All of these challenges would play out over the next five years and at times put the college's future in jeopardy. Even with an uncertain future, leaders and staff at the college dedicated themselves to the task at hand, believing that the mission was worth it.

There were some signs of hope along the way—as well as some small encounters that would pay off for the future, even though no one was aware of what they meant at the time.

One of those signs was a result of an incredible miracle in an unlikely place—the men's room at the Minneapolis–St. Paul International Airport.

While waiting for a flight at the Minneapolis airport, ACC long-term volunteer Alan Finifrock ducked into the restroom for a quick pit stop. As he was washing his hands, he struck up a conversation with a man standing at the next sink, who reminded him of a friend from his days in the army.

"Are you going somewhere or coming home?" Finifrock asked, a question he'd often used to strike up a conversation and pass the time while traveling.

"I'm going home," the man replied, adding that he was from Anchorage.

When Finifrock mentioned that he was headed home to Soldotna, the man's eyes brightened. It turned out that he was part of an investment group that owned property in Alaska, including a parcel in Soldotna, kitty-corner from Kenai Peninsula College. What the man did not know was that the property was also right next door and adjacent to Alaska Christian College.

"I have to admit that I don't know a lot about that land," Finifrock recalled the man saying. "But every once in a while, we're down there."

The two exchanged business cards, and once he returned to campus, he handed the man's contact information over to Hamilton, along with what became known as the "urinal miracle"—and was retold for years.

Hamilton took the card and put it in his file but didn't act on it right away.

Years later, however, when the consideration again of building the athletic center (AC) came up, that card came in handy. Hamilton had filed it long ago before he had first began thinking about purchasing the 4.23-acre plot adjacent to the college, which would be a perfect site for the AC. The only trouble was finding out who owned it. Property records at the Kenai Peninsula Borough listed an organization called the Sphynx Group as owning the property—but the address in the Borough's files was no longer valid, something Hamilton found out after a letter he wrote to the Sphynx Group was returned by the post office. The public access records for the property listed no other address, no email, phone, or website for the owners of that plot.

Then Hamilton recalled the card that Finifrock had given him. He pulled it out of his files and gave the owner a call. Not long afterward, the two were standing on the two property lines and Hamilton was pitching the idea of the AC to him.

"We stood right at the entrance to the land looking into his forest and I asked them if he could picture 100 Native students playing basketball in a new gym 24 hours a day," Hamilton recalled in his journal, recounting the negotiations over the property. "He told me to make him an offer and I started low, he started high, and we ended up in the middle at $52,000 and shook hands on it." That's binding in Alaska! Only $12,300 an acre. A MIRACLE! That was the good news. The bad news was that ACC had no funding to pay for it.

The good news was that the college now had an offer on the site for an athletic center. This was a key part of the school's long-term campus plan, which would provide a place for students to play basketball and other games and hold social activities to fill the long winter hours. Many of the students at the school had come from communities where the indoor gym was a center of life for the community and that was missing at ACC. At that time, getting to a gym for a friendly game of hoops involved leaving campus, a challenge since few of the students had cars. Hopefully, an athletic center would also prove a recruiting tool to bring students to campus, as well as a draw for conferences and other groups to come to campus during the summer months.

The bad news was, again, that there was no funding to pay for the property. What's new? When they heard about it, the Ideker Family Foundation, longtime supporters of the college, bought the property, with the idea of holding it until the college could raise the needed funds and sell it to ACC, a process that would take several years. In the end, the Foundation donated the entire piece of land to ACC! A MIRACLE!

With a site for a future athletic center in place, Hamilton and other leaders turned their eyes to the day-to-day work of keeping the college going and meeting the needs of students. After a fairly quiet summer, the school year began again with 40 students on campus in the fall of 2012, about 10 short of what school officials had hoped for, leading to more budget cuts. By the middle of the semester, most were on academic probation, with faculty and staff working hard to help students with their academic struggles.

The college's trustees had also begun a process of working on the workplace culture at ACC after some concerns were raised during a survey by the Best Christian Workplace study ran by a group that helped Christian organizations evaluate their work environment. That study, and the follow-up from it, would lead to months of meetings and a focus on how to build the best organizational structure for the college long term. It seemed most prudent that the president could no longer do all the travel required and stay home to serve the campus fully. Something had to change. The trustees determined it was best to hire an executive vice president to direct and operate the day-to-day needs of the campus community and for the president to continue the visioning, fundraising, and oversee the macro view of the needs of the campus. With amazing support again, the Murdock Trust came through with a three-year grant to hire and equip the new position of an executive vice president for approximately $200,000! A MIRACLE!

An annual fundraising dinner brought in about $60,000 that year, double from 2011, and enough to repay a loan the college had been taken with National Covenant Properties. That allowed college leaders to work on rebuilding the school's cash reserves.

December of 2012 also brought some troubling fiscal realities. Only 26 students had made it to the end of the semester, and five of those students were departing the college for good. Even with 10 new students set to arrive in January the student population remained too low, requiring $200,000 in budget cuts and likely more layoffs to avoid what Hamilton would refer to as a "fiscal cliff."

With the help of end-of-year giving, the college was able to pay its bills, but more fiscal troubles were on the horizon. Adding to the college's challenges was that a long-hoped-for, game-changing, major gift appeared to be falling apart. For months, Hamilton had been talking with a donor whose company was involved with a major international finance project. If the deal went through, the donor hoped to make a gift large enough to set up an endowment for the college. Again, this would be a long-term game changer and likely ensure the college's long-term survival. But that gift, which once seemed imminent, appeared to not be possible in the end.

Even as the school prepared to make significant budget cuts, college leaders were still working on other long-term projects, including a plan to widen the access road, Royal Place, and to put in a bike path along E Poppy Road, both paid for with funds from the State of Alaska and one that would involve partnering with local officials. The sticking point involved getting the college's neighbors to agree to the project, a task that ended up taking several years.

The 2012 school year ended with a small graduation again, with five students completing the first-year certificate, while two more graduated from the second-year degree program. That graduation was followed by a difficult summer where finances were "bad," Hamilton would recount in his journal, with the college missing repeated payroll dates over the summer. While staff would eventually get paid, the college was often more than a week or two weeks behind on repeated occasions.

That fall, 51 students arrived on campus for fall orientation, the largest group in the college's history and a small sign that things might turn around. The students, at least in the early stages, appeared to be thriving academically and the semester started on a hopeful note. The staff seemed to be rallying around the continuous need for institutional stability.

"We need to settle things down after a year of pushing to (succeed)," Hamilton would write in his journal. "We are the little college that could." In fact, *Christianity Today* would write an entire article about ACC as the "little college that could."

The semester ended with more signs that at least some stability was on the way, including an unexpected $200,000 donation late in the year that allowed the college to end 2013 in the black, no small accomplishment after the previous summer's troubles. The following spring brought news that the State would fund the road widening project and a bike path near the school's entrance, both projects that the college hoped to work on over the next summer. A MIRACLE!

Just before graduation, a letter arrived on campus with the results of the Department of Education's review of ACC's Title III programs. The news was not good. The evaluator ruled that the college had not met the program requirements and therefore was not eligible for Title III funds. In the short term, that meant the school's Title III account, which still contained about $200,000, had been locked, and the staff who worked on the program faced layoffs.

Those funds would eventually be unlocked but the email announcing that the funds were available came with foreboding news. The Department of Education had decided that ACC was not eligible to receive the Title III funds in the first place. They stated that ACC should not been able to receive funds since they weren't accredited at the time of the application. Strangely enough, the entire application for the grant was written for ACC to become accredited and the U.S. Department of Education's grant readers, program officers, and final decision makers knew full well that ACC wasn't accredited yet. Hamilton was told later, in confidence from someone on the inside, that it all began when a new senior program officer at the U.S. Department of Education heard an update on ACC and that they were working toward full accreditation. Her comment to her team was, "What? How can a Christian college receive Title III funding?" Unless the college could provide evidence to the contrary, ACC would have to pay back all $2.2 million of the grant. This, of course, would be a strong and negative game changer for the future of ACC.

"I could not believe what I was reading," Hamilton wrote in his journal, recounting his reaction to the federal Title III email. "This could not only cripple

ACC horrendously, but it could even mean closure if our supporters and God's plan for us did not go our way in support and faith that this mountain cannot be moved."

In the months to come, Hamilton would consult with the college's lawyers, call on Alaska federal officials for help, and do all he could to avoid the calamity that faced the college. Yet the potential possibility existed that the end had come.

The only hope in averting this disaster was getting the Department of Education to reduce the amount of funds that the college would have to repay. In the best-case scenario, essentially forgive the grant, a process that Hamilton would refer to as "non-repayment," was an option that the State's two U.S. senators and congressional representative urged the Department of Education to consider. But while the department rejected the non-repayment option, there was hope that the amount to be repaid could be reduced.

Challenging the Department of Education in court seemed a no-win scenario—costing the college money, time, and energy, all of which were in short supply and would keep college leaders, especially Hamilton, from focusing on how to keep the college open with this enormous distraction.

"My concern is the length to which we would have to go to pay this, the taxing weight on ACC, and my own heart and commitment to fight this," Hamilton wrote in his journal as he deliberated on how to respond. "I am resolved to endure this to the end."

Rather than filing suit, the college began a long, drawn-out process of negotiating with federal officials over how much the school needed to repay. Their first offer was inspired by a college in the lower 48, which had also found itself at odds with the Department of Education—and settled for five percent of what federal officials wanted the school to repay. For ACC that would amount to repaying $110,000 over a period of years.

With the college settled in for a prolonged negotiation and no immediate demand for total repayment to the Department of Education, Hamilton left ACC for a long-planned four-month sabbatical in 2014. His last act before the sabbatical began was to talk with a foundation about a possible matching grant for the proposed athletic center, a proposal that had some promise but would take years to come to fruition.

Hamilton's time away from the college proved a turning point and he returned the following spring re-energized and with a new job description, one focused more on fundraising (about 80 percent of time effort) and less on the day-to-day business of running the college.

He also cut back drastically with his time with the fire department, even though it pained him to do so, and began making plans for what he might do in future years. While only 52, having such a plan gave him some personal goals to aim for, something that founders of ministries often fail to do, to their detriment. It also was one of the first times that Hamilton had begun to think about what ACC might be like when he was gone. While he planned to stay at the school, Lord willing, until his retirement, acknowledging the fact that he one day would leave was also a healthy development. Hamilton also accepted the role as a member of the Trustee Board of North Park University, the denominational college of the Evangelical Covenant Church. He saw the role as a chance to build his network among Covenant leaders, grow awareness of ACC, and give back to the denomination that has so shaped his life since surrendering to Christ at a Covenant camp in 1979.

Hamilton also returned to worries, including a $200,000 budget shortfall and no movement on the negotiations with the Department of Education. And yet, even those headaches seemed overshadowed, at least at the beginning, by all the support the college began to receive after Hamilton's sabbatical, including a weekend of travel to Turlock Covenant Church and Covenant Village, which led to nearly half a million in donations over a series of miracles, including a potential building that could be sold and the profits given to the college. A MIRACLE!

The 2015 commencement also proved a high point, with nine graduates—a welcome turnout from the dwindling numbers in previous years. The following summer brought a few work groups to campus as well as a few rental conferences but no major changes to the campus. Instead, Hamilton and other leaders focused on longer-term projects, including plans for a proposed partnership with the Alaska Mental Health Trust to develop a new associate's degree in mental health as well as developing more support for the New Hope Counseling Center and perhaps for the AC project. College leaders also began preliminary work on a new residence hall that would allow the college to house as many as 45 additional students, a real possibility, given that 75 students enrolled on campus in the fall of 2015, the largest student body in the college's history. By the start of the second semester, that number had dropped to 60, which was still a sign of success, given that the college had never had one semester, let alone two in a row, with more than 50 students on campus.

To promote the new residence hall, which had been christened the "Taikuu" ("thanks" in Inupiat) project, Hamilton hoped to recruit about three dozen donors to give $20,000 each and then to raise the rest from foundations and other major donors. The million-dollar project would be one of the largest in the college's history, and a step of faith, given the uncertainty around the Title III funds.

After 18 months of delay, the Department of Education rejected the college's proposal to reduce the amount of money the school owned and insisted instead that the college had the means to repay the entire $2.2 million balance. The Department also asked Hamilton to put together a repayment schedule. Eventually, the college's Board of Trustees would take over responsibility for deciding how to respond, freeing up Hamilton to focus on the new dorm project.

Although the news about the Title III grant continued to be devastating, fundraising for the dorm project was going well, with more than a dozen donors signing up by early 2016 to donate $20,000 each for the project, with another $100,000 pledged in the form of a challenge grant. Those initial grants would open the door for a major foundation request to complete the project, which seemed to be moving closer to becoming a reality. By May, more than half a million had been raised for the project in designated funds.

The 2016 academic year flew by with six students graduating that May. That was followed by more than 60 rural Indigenous high school students arriving on campus for a month-long program run by Alaska EXCEL, a nonprofit that helps students from rural communities gain career and college-prep skills. The program provided $100,000 in rental income in addition to giving the students a first-hand look at the college. ACC could not afford to ever fly 60 rural Indigenous students to campus, and yet, here was a program that sent them to ACC for a full month and paid entirely for it! A MIRACLE!

That summer, the Department of Education also asked the college for a copy of the college's financial report, which showed that the college ended the year with a deficit of about $25,000. The Department of Education also gave the college an August 31 deadline to come up with a new repayment proposal, with the school's leaders planning to once again offer to pay five percent of the total due. A decision on the counterproposal, which could determine whether ACC had a long-term future or not, would be planned for early November.

"We wait, pray, and fast," Hamilton wrote in his journal.

The summer brought more workers to campus as well as some good news, an unexpected gift of $167,000 from the estate of a donor, on top of a previous $110,000 that had come in just before the end of the fiscal year, let the campus breathe again. The staff restructuring, which freed Hamilton up to fundraise and put the day-to-day operations in the hands of the staff, seemed to be paying off as well. Not only was the new residence project well underway but recruiting for the college remained strong, with more than 80 students, a new record, arriving on campus for the fall of 2016.

In October, the college celebrated 15 years of ministry, with more than 200 people gathering in the campus conference center for a meal of salmon, halibut, and tri-tip steaks, accompanied by songs and dances from the students. That was followed by a groundbreaking for the new residence hall and the presentation of an award to Jeff Siemers, the school's longest-tenured employee aside from Hamilton.

"I have been the blessed recipient of Jeff's wisdom, strength, labor of love, and companionship since July of 2001," Hamilton wrote in reflecting on Siemers' tenure at the college.

Following the celebration, the college received a final copy of its audit for the 2016 fiscal year, which had been delayed, which led to the school asking for more time to present its Title III counteroffer. Still, school officials hoped to hear back from the Department of Justice, who had taken up their case after Education had made their decision, by the end of the year.

The beginning of 2017 brought an outpouring of support for the college, with an annual dinner raising more than $55,000. Total pledges and gifts for the new Taikuu Residence Hall had topped more than a million dollars, with another major foundation matching grant pending. The success of the fundraising for the dorm freed up Hamilton to focus on operational funding, an ongoing challenge, with the school needing to dip into reserves to make payroll in May.

In May of 2017, the college held the largest graduation in its history, with a dozen students earning degrees—another milestone and sign of the impact that the college was having in the lives of students. Almost as soon as the students had left, volunteer work crews began arriving with more than 400 Sowers on campus that summer (largest in ACC's history) to begin work on the new hall, which made room for more students to experience the life-changing community the college could offer.

By the end of the summer, more good news arrived, in the form of an email from the Department of Education. Rather than reading it on the computer screen, Hamilton printed out the message and then gathered the staff in the school's computer lab for prayer. Then he read the message aloud, learning for the first time that the Department of Education offered to settle the matter for $250,000, or about one-tenth of what the Department claimed was owed. The college would be given five years to repay at nearly zero interest and could still receive other federal aid dollars as long as they remained on time with the payment plan.

"My first and immediate response was a sense of relief," Hamilton would later write. "The college is saved." A MIRACLE!

By the grace of God and the extreme goodness of a family that heard of the opportunity to pay off all of ACC's debt related to the classroom building portion of the $250,000 due, they wrote a very generous check to pay off all of the debt owed to the U.S. Department of Education within months, not years! A MIRACLE!

Hamilton would add: "Great and bright days are ahead, I pray. With another record-breaking attendance of 84 students, we are blessed and excited to take the challenge before us to the Lord of Lords. We will soon be firing on all cylinders to the glory of God."

ACC students and staff share native dress.

ACC students proudly shared their native traditions.

More students enjoying the Kenai Peninsula.

ACC students doing a native cultural dance.

Students built strong connections through shared experiences on campus.

Students built strong connections through shared experiences on campus.

Students built strong connections through shared experiences on campus.

Hands-on learning was an integral part of education at ACC.

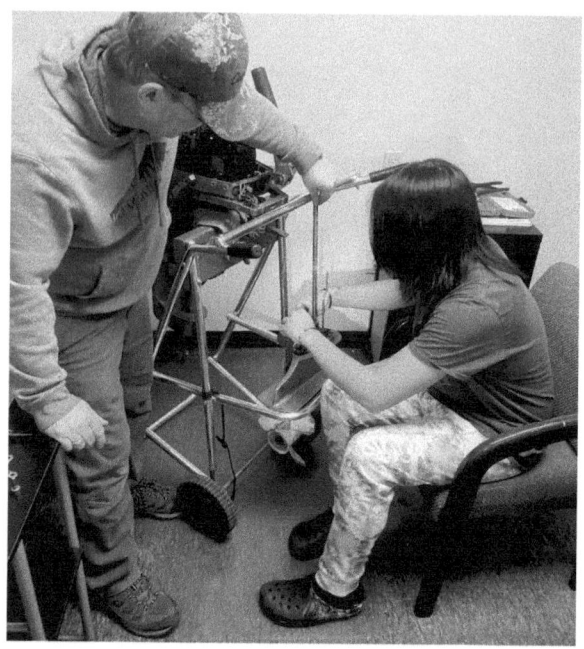

Hands-on learning was an integral part of education at ACC.

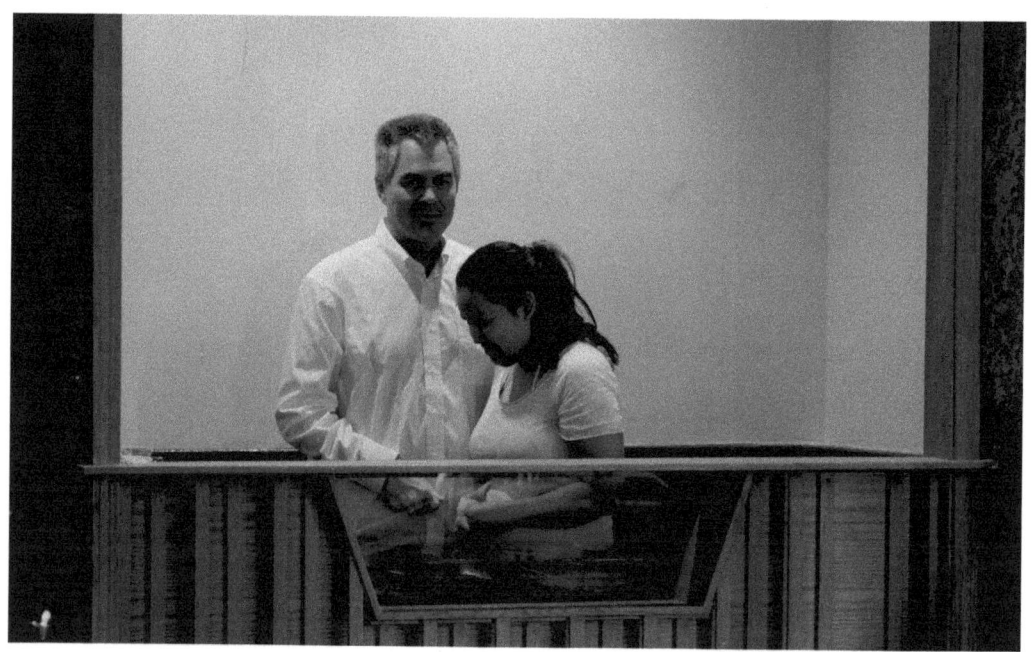

Faith shaped daily life, guiding both personal growth and community values.

Faith shaped daily life, guiding both personal growth and community values.

Graduation 2025.

Every year, ACC students served in Mexico helping with construction, service, and ministry activities.

The internship program at ACC allowed graduates and others to begin working in a field as they plan for their future.

Second generation student after completing the Yamaha marine motors certification.

The Aarigaa Yurt was completed in 2015. It was used as a large meeting space.

Taikuu Residence Hall (the final addition to the Peninsula Conference Center) completed in 2018.

Dedication of Taikuu Residence Hall in September 2018.

New Hope Counseling Center addition and remodel completed in 2025.

In 2011, ACC won a disability-accessible Toyota Sienna through Toyota's "100 Cars for Good" program.

Campus tour with U.S. Senator and his wife along with ACC alumnus.

Full-time maintenance staff became critical as the campus grew to include 30 acres and 28 building projects.

Athletic Center ground breaking in September 2019.

2024 aerial view of campus.

Ribbon cutting by students at the Athletic Center dedication in September 2024.

Government representatives speak at the Athletic Center dedication.

Students demonstrating Native Youth Olympics at the Athletic Center dedication.

Practicing shots on the court inside the Athletic Center.

Friendly competition during a student basketball game.

A fitness center and locker rooms were added to the Athletic Center in 2025.

9

By the fall of 2017, with the dispute over federal Title III funds settled for the most part and construction of the new Taikuu Residence Hall well on its way, Alaska Christian College settled into a period of steady growth and stability. The existential threat of having to pay back millions to the federal government was gone, though the negotiations on the terms of the final settlement took months to finalize. The president now began to look ahead to the school's upcoming 20th anniversary, an amazing opportunity to give thanks to God in many tangible ways.

Meanwhile, the campus itself was a hive of activity, with volunteers still hard at work on the Taikuu dorm until mid-October, led by volunteers Dennis and Connie Schnicke, Ike Dotomain, and Larry Streiff. There were hopes of opening the dorm up for the spring semester, so that the college would no longer have to turn students away due to a shortage of housing. Though college leaders did not know it at the time, the extra bed space would prove crucial in a few years, when a worldwide pandemic would make social distancing a part of everyday life and a key component of keeping the college open.

Local contractors were also at work paving the parking lot after all the trees were removed, which gave a facelift to the campus, just in time for the arrival of 84 students that fall, another new enrollment record. The college's finances, which for years had been touch and go, were also stabilized, and were strengthened later in the fall by an unexpected donation of $330,000 from a bequest, which helped pay off the final bills from the residence hall as well as much of the college's remaining debt. A MIRACLE!

The conflict over the Title III funds did cause some ongoing headaches, especially with the school's fiscal year 2018 audit, which was delayed as the settlement with the Department of Justice, who had taken over the case, was not finalized. That delay had a domino effect, leading to delays in getting an annual report to the college's accreditors, which could have led to sanctions if not resolved.

Student loans also proved an ongoing challenge, as the default rate for ACC students passed the 30 percent mark, meaning students could lose access to future loans as well as Pell Grants and other financial aid if the default rate did not improve. The concerns with loans led to a discussion of the need to develop an endowment for the college, one that would generate the quarter of a million dollars annually that student loans filled in the college's budget.

The default rate ended up reaching 39.8 percent for the rolling three-year-old cohort finally. At 40 percent, ACC would lose all of its federal loan program and the Pell grant program, which by itself produced $750,000 a year in revenue against student costs of education. This was a crisis that the Board of Trustees and the PAC had been watching closely for some time. Hamilton spent time in communicating with the federal representatives about the issue on more than one occasion. While representing the State of Alaska at an educational conference in Washington, DC, Hamilton saw that Betsy DeVos, the U.S. Secretary of Education, was a keynote speaker at his conference. Following the event, Hamilton followed her off of the stage into the hallway, stepping carefully in front of her (and her security), to ask if he could have three minutes of her time as the President of ACC. She paused, then agreed to allow him to speak with her as she headed to her car. He shared with her the concern over the default rate issue and she passed him over to her handler who said she would definitely look into it.

Unbeknownst to Hamilton, U.S. Senator Dan Sullivan had personally called Secretary DeVos to request a two-year extension for ACC to prove their ability to recover from their 39.8 percent default rate before losing access to Pell grants.

Further, U.S. Senator Lisa Murkowski had her office research other options. One other state had a Native-based college also with the same dilemma, and they made a law change that was only applicable to that situation that was sunk deep into U.S. legislation. Hamilton used the same language, changed the name of schools, and submitted it to the Senator's office. The day before the omnibus bill was to be signed, ACC's language had been stripped by the House of Representative's version. Hamilton was told there was no chance for it to be reinserted back into the bill. The day following the president's signing of the bill, Hamilton got an unexpected call from the senator's office liaison telling him that, in fact, the bill *did* include the ACC language to waive all the default rate problems up to that point. Their liaison was incredulous, not knowing how in the world it made it through when it was absent just before it went to the president's desk the day before. A MIRACLE!

The 2018 spring semester opened with a healthy enrollment—75 students on campus—and meetings with the college's board, where a new VISION 2020 capital campaign was approved. The majority of the capital campaign was built around the long-running dream of an athletic center on campus, a dream that seemed to be moving closer to reality.

> VISION 2020 was focused on sustainability and included three goals: building out the campus with an athletic center and classroom addition, growing the Legacy Endowment to provide more scholarship funds, and setting aside funds for future sustainability.

May brought another graduation, with eight students completing degrees, including the first graduate in the college's new Associates in Behavioral Health degree program. That was followed by a relatively quiet summer, with a few work teams and the return of the Alaska Native student EXCEL program, which brought in much-needed rental income. Some of those students would become ACC students in the coming years.

The fall of 2018 once again began with record enrollment, 94 students on campus, many of them housed in the new Taikuu dorm, which was dedicated in mid-September. Having that many students on campus brought new challenges and taxed some of the support services that the college offered, but was a sign that students were seeing the school's value.

The fall of 2018 also brought the culture wars over the place of religion in American culture, once again to Soldotna. Although the college was not at the center of the debate, this time the conflict was over who could give invocations at the local Kenai Peninsula Borough Assembly meetings. As the leader of a local institution, Hamilton had a front-row view of the debates and was the key person in the work to resolve this issue.

Those debates had been going on since at least 2016 when a member of the so-called Satanic Temple, an activist group that believed prayers of public meetings and other government-related expressions of faith are unconstitutional, gave an invocation that ended with "Hail Satan," the group's catchphrase. That led to public backlash and an attempt to replace the invocation at regular meetings with a moment of silence.

Much of the debate revolved around the assembly's rules for determining who could pray at meetings and who could not, rules that were eventually deemed unconstitutional by the Alaska Supreme Court. They argued that government officials should not be determining which religious groups were valid and which were not. That led the Kenai Peninsula Borough Assembly to pass new rules, which Hamilton supported, which allowed prayers to continue. His hope, as Hamilton wrote in his journal, was that Christians in the community would be active in the community and pay attention to what happened in local politics as concerned community members. Hamilton continues to this day to bring invocations at a regular variety of community events, government gatherings, and clubs. With humility, he also annually spends a few days meeting to pray with many legislators and the Governor in Juneau, Alaska's capitol, during the legislative session, including hosting a pizza and prayer dinner event with the legislature.

As the new year began, the college received news that two ACC friends, Chris Anderson (PAC member) and his son-in-law, Luke Ringenberg (current ACC Trustee), wanted to introduce Hamilton to friends of theirs that owned a construction company in Vancouver, Washington. This would be the first ask to a donor for a matching challenge gift to the VISION 2020 campaign. Hamilton had never met this donor who had been a $5,000-a-year donor for two decades.

He was just a friend who did business with Anderson and Ringenberg's company, Lamwood, out of Denver. With a box of salmon, halibut, prawns, and scallops in hand, Hamilton traveled to Vancouver, Washington, to meet up at the office of the donor with Anderson and Ringenberg. Much to Hamilton's surprise, when he gifted the seafood meat package gift to the donor, he found out that they were Seventh-day Adventists and did not eat meat! Lesson number one in fundraising, "Know your donor!" Hamilton wrote in his journal, with a bit of self-deprecating humor.

The donor had given large gifts to the college in the past, including $250,000 for the new classroom addition on campus as a part of the settlement with the U.S. Department of Education.

The timing was perfect. The family's foundation was under a deadline to give away all of its funds by 2020, and they were looking for worthwhile projects to support and Hamilton had just begun fundraising for the VISION 2020 project. All he had in hand was a primary draft of the brochure for the capital campaign. The family in particular was interested in funding the college's new athletic center and made the first major gift to the $5 million total campaign. The day after the visit, Anderson got a call from the donor who challenged ACC with this: if ACC can raise $1 million in four months, they would match the $1 million! Game on! As Christmas was approaching, it was best to wait until the first of the year to earnestly raise the challenge amount. Hamilton's first request was to the President's Advisory Council, then to the Board of Trustees, and finally to the staff and faculty of ACC. In all, 99 total people pledged or contributed in cash just over $1.2 million! A MIRACLE!

In addition, once again, the MJ Murdock Trust contributed a whopping $500,000 gift, the largest in their history to ACC. And, for its first major gift, the Rasmuson Foundation of Anchorage, Alaska, granted $400,000 to the athletic center project! When you add the $1.2 million that the 99 raised, $1 million from the Vancouver donor, and the two foundations, all of the $3 million toward the AC part of the campaign had been raised in a period of less than a year! A MIRACLE! The remainder of the campaign to reach the $5 million total would take another year for the other goals, with final results surpassing the goal amount. With increased material costs due to COVID-19, approximately $5.5 million was raised in total. Praise God! A MIRACLE!

Much of 2019 was focused on raising funds for the capital program, with Hamilton spending much of his time out on the road, meeting with donors, with a trip to Washington, DC for the National Prayer Breakfast as well as a meeting with the Department of Education officials about the college's student loan default rate. By the fall, more than $3.2 million had been raised for the capital campaign.

That fall also marked record enrollment for the college, with 105 students arriving for the first day of classes, a new high-water mark. Alaska Christian College appeared well on its way to a new era of stability and growth. The capital campaign seemed destined for success, with work on the new AC set to begin the following summer.

The first signs, however, that things were changing, came in early March of 2020. The set agenda for a long-planned meeting of the school's Presidential Advisory Council, beginning on March 13, was scrapped as college leaders found themselves facing an unprecedented challenge, the full arrival of COVID-19. Already there were signs of how the pandemic would disrupt life, even in rural Alaska, as relatively few of the PAC members made it to campus, due to concerns about the virus.

By Saturday, March 14, it was clear that the campus—like schools across the country—would have to close in the coming week. However, when he received news that Hooper Bay was closing to outsiders coming in, he called the President's Cabinet together late on Tuesday the 17th. It was clear students needed to leave *now*. This decision, as Hamilton would later recount, left students distraught, angry, and frightened and left staff scrambling to find ways to get the students home. They had three hours to pack. Many left by van, in a heavy snowstorm, for the airport in Anchorage at 1 a.m., where they then caught 6 a.m. flights home on Alaska Airlines (only on standby) and Ravn Alaska, which specializes in travel to remote villages. Others went by ACC vans to home communities on the road system, while a few left by snow machine after getting to their hub villages.

By the end of the week, 90 percent of the students had headed home. Many of the students returning to rural villages were faced with two weeks in quarantine before they could be exposed to the other villagers. This local decision, made by elders in the villages, was due to the memory of the previous pandemic in the early 1900s that decimated several villages when the disease spread rapidly in small communities. Some students were unable to return home, at least not immediately, and ended up living with ACC staff and other college supporters in the area like Bethel and Nome, hub travel communities.

Sixteen of the college's staffers, mostly those working in food service and in residence life, were laid off, as there were no students for them to work for. Most of them received two weeks' severance pay and were eligible for COVID-related unemployment benefits as well as the college starting a benevolence fund to help staffers affected by the layoffs.

The college also applied for a small business loan through the Payroll Protection Program to keep other staff on campus, while the college also received funds from the Department of Education, which were used to refund the unused room and board fees students had paid and to begin converting the college to online education.

It was no easy process.

"Distance education has been hard," Hamilton would later write in his journal. "We sent home books, thumb drives, and Kindles to assist students. We have paid for cell phones, added to bandwidth, hot spot option, and are doing classes via Zoom. Our staff and faculty have been pulling up their bootstraps in a huge way!"

Of particular concern were the 15 students who were set to graduate that spring, which would have been the largest graduating class in the school's history. Now staff worried about what might happen to them in this transition to online education. For the short-term at least, graduation was postponed for the foreseeable future, as Soldotna, like communities around the country, was on lockdown in hopes of limiting the harm done by COVID-19.

By April, the challenges of online education in Alaska, especially very limited internet, and the complication caused by the lockdown were already taking their toll on students at ACC. Eighteen students needed to take "Incompletes" as classes wrapped up for the semester. The best provider of internet was the local K-12 school. With them also closed, the students had hardly any bandwidth available to Zoom calls. Fortunately, 14 students ended up graduating, though with little fanfare and none of the celebrations that had marked the previous years' commencements.

In August, however, the college would hold a late and delayed in-person graduation at Peninsula Grace Church, which was also broadcast on Zoom, with nine of the graduating students being able to attend. Some of the students were also able to go camping the days before graduation at the nearby Diamond M Ranch to give closure to the school year that they never received on campus.

Back on campus, Rev. Sean Hoffbeck, the longtime vice president for operations, began work on a "reopen the campus" task force, charged with preparing the school for the fall. The plan for reopening included renting dorm space at nearby Kenai Peninsula College, as every student needed to have their own room in order to maintain social distancing. The college also moved to an online model for classes, which required a costly upgrade to the campus's internet service. Fortunately, grants were immediately available to pay for all the upgrades.

The Sowers work groups for June mostly self-canceled, even though Alaska was early to reopen from lockdowns. A few dozen showed up that summer from Rolling Hills Covenant Church, Rolling Hills Estates, California, and He's Alive Church, Kannapolis, North Carolina. Due to this, most of the planned projects were put on hold. Instead, both volunteers and staff turned their attention to preparing the site for the athletic center with the help of the use of a bulldozer, grader, dump truck, and other heavy machinery ready for the initial groundwork.

Despite the challenges of COVID-19, 50 first-year students arrived on campus that fall, along with about 40 returning students, putting enrollment down about 15 percent from the previous year. A number of the COVID-19 precautions, spreading the students over two campuses, practicing social distancing at meals and inside, as well as holding some classes online, appeared to help hold down the impact of COVID-19 on campus. There never was any widespread outbreak on campus.

As the school year began, working on the AC site continued, though work on the capital campaign had mostly stalled due to the need to focus on COVID-19 funding. Hamilton had been told initially that the groundwork would likely need about six inches of gravel for the cement pad. Final engineering estimates put it, instead, at four feet for all 28,000 sqaure feet needed! With only $20,000 budgeted for the pad, Hamilton invited Doug Norris, the neighbor behind ACC that owned a gravel pit, for lunch at ACC.

At lunch, around the table of the "Grumpy Old Men," Hamilton described the need for the very best price that Doug could offer. After some calculations, the quote was $400,000! Ouch. Then Doug, a fellow Christian, leaned over to Hamilton and said, "You know, I don't like giving away business, but your land butts up against my land and you have the same gravel on your side of the line that I do, why don't you just mine your own gravel?" Hamilton was astonished as he wasn't aware this was an option, but, surely, it was. Doug also offered the use of his bulldozer and compactor at no charge, though the college would have to recruit heavy equipment operators to run them. In addition, more equipment would be needed, so Hamilton purchased an excavator for $56,000 from raised funds, borrowed a second excavator, and a dump truck.

It was so slow going with one excavator at one end, the other at the AC site, and just one dump truck, that a volunteer from Minnesota left one afternoon early from the work site. Why? He went into town and bought a $10,000 used dump to donate to the college and double the effort of moving all the gravel to its new location. Then, Dennis Schnicke, the head volunteer contractor for the project, told Hamilton the project needed a loader, not only for the AC construction, but also for the heavy snow that would need to be removed from the very large parking lot on campus. Hamilton told Schnicke that the budget had no money for a loader in it. Schnicke commented that he had found one that a church friend owned and the price was $45,000. "Unless someone called to buy us a loader, it would have to wait," said Hamilton. Within an hour, Hamilton's phone rang. It was from a couple in Washington who had been doing their morning devotions and were praying for ACC. They asked if ACC needed anything. Without hesitation, Hamilton said, "A loader!" When the couple responded that they would be interested, Hamilton asked them how much they could place towards a down payment to get it to campus ASAP. They committed $20,000 on the spot but actually sent $25,000! A MIRACLE! This left $20,000 left to raise.

As this gift was the end of one calendar year, Hamilton contacted the family again in the new calendar year, asking if they would like to buy *all* of the loader. The response a few days later was thrilling—the couple would give $5,000, their son and daughter would do the same, and their grandson would donate crypto to make up the difference. A MIRACLE! It is interesting to note that this same family was descendants of Covenant missionaries who served in the early 1900s in southeast Alaska. Legacy giving at its best!

Eventually, over the COVID-19 summer of 2020, over 400 loads of gravel would be used to make the base for the new building, all coming from ACC's own gravel pit. The cost to that entire step in the building process? It was less than the $20,000 originally budgeted! A MIRACLE!

That same fall, the college also dedicated the new classroom expansion as a part of the VISION 2020 campaign, a 3,000 square foot building with a pair of state-of-the-art classrooms, a third classroom for Behavioral Health courses, and six offices for faculty. The college also welcomed Jeff and Andrea Smith, a family of former missionaries from Turkey, to the staff. Jeff was hired to oversee the brand new $2 million Title III grant, this one fortunately without the kind of issues that caused so much trouble with federal officials in the past. Andrea would become the new Director of Financial Aid after Krista Pitsch successfully ended her 17 years of service to ACC with her most recent role as Director of Financial Aid and Enrollment. Under her service, she recruited ACC's largest classes in recent years.

Academically, many of the students struggled to adapt to the COVID-19 restrictions that limited their access to classrooms, the library, and face-to-face contact with staff. As many as half the students were struggling to pass their classes. Returning students had a difficult time adapting to the new realities. The semester ended with two students, Minnie Harris and Tessa Coopchiak, graduating on Zoom before students dispersed for the holidays.

The summer of 2021 brought more work on the AC, including negotiations with the City of Soldotna for a fire hydrant to bring city water to the campus. Doing so meant that the city would annex the property, which was currently outside the city limits. ACC was not desiring to leave the Borough and enter the city when the discovery work showed the cost and time effort to be way too long in the future to keep the project moving forward. It was decided by Hamilton that an above-the-ground, 17,500 gallon water tank would be the best answer in how to carry reserves for the sprinkler system in the AC.

The first bill for the building's steel frame arrived that summer as well, $170,000 of nearly $500,000 needed for the girders that made up the frame and the steel panels that would construct the building's exterior walls. That bill, while high, was lower than expected. Steel prices, like the cost of all other building materials, had skyrocketed during COVID. ACC local friend, Dick Ruckman, who owned the local company that sold the college the steel at his cost, did so with the price that was first negotiated in 2020 before the pandemic began. Of course, prices went up

30 percent on steel and Hamilton contacted Dick to ask what could be done. Dick contacted the steel manufacturer in Visalia, California, and the concern went up their corporate chain until a Christian boss determined that they could afford to keep the price at the pre-pandemic level! A MIRACLE! The steel was set to arrive on campus by the end of summer of 2021, which would give staff at the college a year to continue working on preparing the site and pouring the foundation. Along with the price of steel skyrocketing everywhere (except ACC), so did the transportation of the steel from California to Alaska. It had to be trucked from Visalia, California, to Seattle, Washington, then barged to Anchorage, and trucked down to Soldotna. Hamilton spoke with State Senate President Peter Micciche, a longtime friend of ACC and the Hamiltons, about his connections with the barge carriers and if ACC could receive a discount. With his support and willingness to ask, seven of the 11 barge loads of steel were completely donated to ACC, saving tens of thousands of dollars for the project. The remainder loads were provided at a discounted price. A MIRACLE!

In April of 2021, the college celebrated its 20th commencement, with a dozen students graduating, all in caps, gowns, and face masks, a reminder of all they had been through. The college also had enough funding so that no students had to take out student loans for 2020 or 2021, a welcome relief for both students and staff. A MIRACLE!

The college's academic programs also received a boost when the State decided to allow students to transfer credits to the University of Alaska system. That summer, the first graduate of the college was able to transfer her credits to the University of Alaska at Fairbanks. This effort of transfer of credit was the outcome of Hamilton's volunteer board service on the Alaska State Board of Education and as a commissioner on the Alaska Commission on Post-secondary Education. He was able to encourage both entities to sign on to resolutions he wrote that would be approved and sent to both the governor's office and the chancellors of the University of Alaska system. Both he and ACC's vice president of academics worked to secure this accomplishment after dead-end attempts for over 20 years for this transfer of credit. How crazy it was that an ACC professor, Dr. Steve Hallam, who taught the exact same math class at both ACC and KPC, did so without the class being transferable until this articulation agreement was completed.

"We have finally made it to the big leagues," Hamilton would write in his journal.

Despite the few cases of COVID-19 on campus, there was fallout from the pandemic, largely in the drop-off in enrollment. For the spring of 2022, enrollment stood at 75 students, down 25 percent from just two years earlier, a sign of things to come. Engagement was down as well, with fewer and fewer students involved in social activities and in the spiritual life of the college.

"We are needing a reboot, a spiritual reboot through a time of prayer and fasting," Hamilton would later write in his journal. "If we could take away DoorDash and add an athletic center, things would look different for sure!"

The college's finances remained stable in 2022, in part because a number of longtime supporters had added bequests to the college in their wills. Among them was Dick Becker, a friend of Hamilton, who died in December of 2021, not long after visiting with Hamilton for a "Taste of Alaska" event in Florida for supporters of the college. The following spring, the college received word that $453,000, all his assets, had been given to the college in Becker's will. Dick joined so many other faithful stewards who gave both in their life here and also their life after "graduating" to heaven. A MIRACLE!

That gift, as most all bequests do, went to the college's small-but-growing endowment, which had grown to about $2 million. The college was also able to contribute about a half-million dollars in reserve to pay off much of its long-term debt in 2022, leaving the school in the strongest financial position in its history with only $250,000 remaining in long-term debt. In May of 2022, both Hamilton and Eric Johnson, Vice President for Advancement, believed that the remaining debt could go away if they would call 20 donors with the opportunity to completely erase the college's debt. When those calls were over, all of the funds had been raised and, during the ensuing Board of Trustees and PAC meetings, ACC was able to burn its mortgage from National Covenant Properties and do the Dave Ramsey debt scream, "We're debt free!" A MIRACLE!

April of 2022 brought a packed house for the graduation banquet, followed by a full house at Peninsula Grace Church to celebrate the nine students who graduated that year.

A wave of volunteers again arrived that summer to work on the new athletic center, in addition to constructing the doubling of office spaces for New Hope

Counseling Center, again, because of the vision of Forest Park Covenant Church, Muskegon, Michigan, and Richard Borgeson. Also, renovations to the main administration building took place with a large facelift to the Denali Room. It was now the same floor height as the upcoming new Student Engagement Center being built behind it with Title III funds.

The summer of 2023 brought more workers to campus, with the shell of the AC finally beginning to rise. How exciting it was to see the frame of how large this structure actually was!

"I hosted the largest teams of the summer last week, 42 volunteers total. Over the summer, 220 volunteers were here. They all made the campus look beautiful," Hamilton wrote in July of 2023. "The AC is moving along quickly with it being enclosed so no rain can impact it and the outer part of the building being sided has helped." By God's providence, just three days shy of a full foot of snow that would stay all year, the roof was completed in the nick of time. Instead of the usual route of doing the sides first, then the roof, Dennis Schnicke changed course to complete the roof before the sides. If this hadn't been the choice, all year long, the local volunteers would have had to work in a foot of snow inside the shell of the AC. A MIRACLE! In addition, hundreds of ravens had nested and pooped all winter long, as the sides were not completely finished to the top of the structure due to safety concerns. Unfortunately, a handful of volunteers had to spend three weeks scraping poop off of the rafters before inside painting could begin.

By the fall of 2023, just under 70 students had arrived on campus, down again from the previous year and part of an ongoing post-COVID trend. The school had hoped to enroll 75 students and began the year with a $175,000 deficit for tuition, one which would likely grow as the year rolled on. The deficit and the departure of some staff meant that only adjunct faculty along with two full-time faculty remained on campus, pressing Debbie Hamilton and other staff into teaching duties.

By the time May of 2024 rolled around, there was good news and bad news on the campus. Campus enrollment had continued to decline. Yet that May, the college graduated its second largest class in the school's history—thirteen students in all, who walked across the stage at Peninsula Grace Church, to the cheers of family and friends.

Dr. Nora Nagurak, an ACC trustee and board secretary, a physician from Nome who grew up in Unalakleet, gave the commencement address. A cancer survivor and life-long Covenanter, Nagurak urged graduates to take what they had learned out to their communities, in service of God and their culture.

"Just like God designed every part of our bodies to have a function, He created us as unique individuals, with unique gifts, placing us in specific times and places in the world, so that He may be glorified," she told graduates.

A few months later, on September 27, 2024, board members, the PAC, students, and a host of honored guests returned to the campus, this time to celebrate the opening of the college's athletic center. This $3.5 million project, including $150,000 to pave the parking lot recently provided by a grant from the Murdock Trust, more than two decades in the planning, had been built primarily by volunteers and the goodwill of local contractors and others willing to give to the cause. It was, as Hamilton has long described, a building of miracles itself, beginning with that chance meeting in the Minneapolis airport, the story now immortalized on a plaque hanging in the newly completed athletic center outside the bathrooms; the story that has been carried through the years as a reminder of God's answer to prayers and faithful giving.

"I want to ask you, dear friends, do you believe that God maybe wanted us to have an athletic center on the campus of Alaska Christian College after all these miracles?" Hamilton asked those gathered for the dedication, as the *Peninsula Clarion*, a local newspaper, reported. All the audience, including the Lt. Governor of Alaska, mayors and legislators, yelled with a resounding answer in unison, *Yes!*

10

The first Board of Trustees for the college was drawn mostly from members of the task force that had been working on developing the idea of the college starting in the late 1990s. Jon Payne from Mat-Su Covenant Church in Wasilla, about an hour north of Anchorage, was the first chair of the board, while Joel Caldwell, a local pilot and founder of Arctic Barnabas Ministries, a ministry that provided care and encouragement for pastors and leaders in rural Alaska, signed on as vice chair. Paul Wilson, then-Field Director for the Covenant's work in Alaska, and Keith Hamilton served on the board ex officio, meaning they were members of the board due to their positions. Rev. Neil Josephson, the president of Covenant Bible College, and a longtime mentor for Hamilton and other college leaders, also joined the board.

In the matter of governance, Alaska Christian College was established as an entity within the Evangelical Covenant Church of Alaska. It has its own Board of Trustees, a 501(c)(3) non-profit designation, Constitution, and Bylaws. The college carries accreditation with the Association for Biblical Higher Education, Orlando, Florida, and is authorized by the Alaska Commission on Postsecondary Education as a college. Further, the Alaska Regional Conference of the Evangelical Covenant Church is the sole Member of ACC, meaning that they hold reserved powers over ACC, including the hiring and removal of the president, any change of bylaws and constitution, and the approval or dismissal of trustees.

In the early years, the Board of Directors (now called trustees) had eight members and no committees. They all met in person a few times a year. This was long before Zoom and other video conferencing technology was available which can make more frequent meetings possible. Having no committees meant that all board members were involved in the oversight of each of the college's programs and all the decisions. That would change in the future as the board grew and the college's programs became more complex.

"It was all face to face," said Hamilton, in recalling the board's early years. "We were pretty unorganized; we didn't know exactly what we were doing."

As the board members and Hamilton gained experience, the board became more organized and efficient with more focus on having a set agenda, and more collaboration between the board and the staff. It was also part of the learning process.

From the beginning, there was a focus on making sure the board reflected the population of the Covenant church (60 percent minimum of members) and the students the college was serving. Alaska Native voices were crucial in this, and one of the school's early supporters was Nathan Toots, a longtime Covenant pastor and former associate field director for the Covenant in Alaska, would eventually become the school's first Native chair. The goal of the board was to have half of the officers and members be Indigenous members.

As the board grew, most board members were Alaskans but some were members from other parts of the lower 48 Covenant states. Trevor Simpson, a former intern of Hamilton's from Colorado, would become the second board chair, and other Covenant leaders, such as Paul Hawkinson, the former treasurer for the Evangelical Covenant Church; Rob Hall, Esq., who worked on real estate issues for the denomination; and Tim Ciccone, a Covenant pastor and former director of the Covenant's national youth ministry, who has been a longtime supporter of ACC, also served on the board. Both Hawkinson and Ciccone would eventually serve as board chairs.

Board of Trustees Chairs
Jon Payne - 11/2000
Trevor Simpson - 11/2004
Rev. Nathan Toots - 11/2006
Rev. Hugh Forbes - 11/2008
Acting chair - Stephanie Eklund 2013
Rev. Scott Merriner - 10/2014
Paul Hawkinson - 11/2018
Rev. Tim Ciccone - 11/2022

As the board and college grew, so did the need to divide the work into committees. The board, which can have a maximum of 19 members, added a personnel committee, finance committee, governance committee, academic committee, and advancement committee to allow board members to give more focus to specific areas. The advent of Zoom and other technologies has allowed those committees to meet more often, while the whole board meets in person twice a year overnight, usually on campus. Those meetings begin with a prayer walk, committees, business meetings all day Friday and Saturday, interspersed with meals and gatherings with students, so the board members can hear about the impact of the college's program. Friday night is usually spent at the Hamilton home with dessert and student testimonies, always a highlight of the weekend. Then, board members are sent home Saturday afternoon, with those from the lower 48 often catching red-eye flights from Anchorage.

Most of the board members live in Alaska, with about a quarter of board members from the lower 48 states. Board leaders have made a concerted effort to add members with specific expertise, especially attorneys, academic personnel, and those with human resource and personnel experience, to help support and guide the staff. In addition, two members must be Covenant licensed/ordained clergy to keep the ministry spiritually focused. The board has also remained focused on adding as many points of view as possible, making sure to have strong Native voices on the board as well as a mix of men and women on the board so that the board somewhat resembles the student body. The board always needs to reflect ACC's constituency.

Tim Ciccone, the current board chair, said serving on the board grew out of his longtime support for the college. Both he and Hamilton share a long interest and commitment to youth ministry in the Covenant and in helping young people grow in their faith. Ciccone taught at the college several times as an adjunct and joined the board in 2019, just months before the start of the COVID-19 pandemic.

Ciccone called serving on the board an "honor" in a 2025 interview, where he praised the level of leadership and commitment shown by board members and staff. "It's been such a joy to learn from them, to really dig into hard conversations over the years and, you know, try to solve the issues that are in front of us, and to support Keith as best we can, and to see all along what God is doing," Ciccone said.

Early on in its history, the school moved from a Board of Directors model, which had been more hands-on, to a Board of Trustees model focused on big-picture policies and issues. As chair, Ciccone travels to Soldotna twice a year for board meetings and responds to a host of emails in between those meetings. Most all of the board's focus is on the larger issue of governance and setting policy, rather than managing the day-to-day operations of the college. Board members set the policies and then the college staff is responsible for carrying them out.

"We have one employee as a Board of Trustees, and that is the president," Ciccone said.

The board is also charged with making the college adhere to its accreditation standards, dealing with budgetary issues, and discussing the long-term vision for the college. Since the pandemic, part of that discussion has been over what kinds of programs the college could offer in the future to meet the needs of students. COVID-19 had profound impacts on how students view education and on how colleges operate and the board is still working through that.

"The board has, over the last couple of years, really worked through what is the model that we need to engage in that can give the school a future," Ciccone said in the early 2025 interview.

Part of the discussion about the future has included starting a new committee to oversee the college's marketing and enrollment, given that COVID-19 brought with it a drop in enrollment. The hope, Ciccone said, is the focus on "trying to find new ways to reach this new generation of students, so that the student enrollment numbers can go back up."

When looking for new members, the board is intentional about including Native leaders, which is essential given the school's focus and its context in the Alaskan church. Getting board members who have had experience in church leadership, such as with the Alaska conference or with Covenant Youth of Alaska (CYAK) continues to be crucial, said Ciccone.

Because of his connections in the Alaskan church and the broader denomination, Hamilton has taken a lead role in recruiting board members for much of the college's history. That's changed recently, in part because the board has begun planning for the longer-term future and an eventual succession with the school's president.

"We are trying to take that responsibility off of Keith's plate, knowing that Keith won't be at ACC forever," Ciccone said. "And so when Keith is gone, what will the standards be for recruiting different board members? The board is taking more and more responsibility in that and hopefully, as the next couple years march on, we'll see that fully move over to the board, where Keith's advising more than doing all the recruiting."

A solid grounding in faith has remained essential for board members, giving the college's values and mission as a Christian institution. "If you're not committed to the call of Christ, it'd be really difficult serving on our board," Ciccone said.

Ciccone said the board is also looking for members with specific skills like finances and advancement, as well as experience working in higher education. The idea is to make sure the board members have the right skills and gifts to oversee the college's programs and future. All board members are also expected to give financially in support of the college.

The board also works to make sure the college remains aligned with the Affirmations and positions of the Evangelical Covenant Church denomination. While students at the college come from all kinds of church traditions (or no church background), the Covenant's ethos and Covenant Affirmations guide how the college expresses and understands the Christian faith.

"Our theological disposition, or how we live out our faith, comes from the broader Covenant family," said Ciccone.

Board and PAC members begin every meeting by reciting the college's mission statement: "The mission of Alaska Christian College is to empower Alaska Natives through biblically-based higher education and Christian formation to pursue excellence in character, learning, and service as followers of Christ." This was adopted as the second mission statement in ACC's history during the process of becoming accredited. It has held the test of time.

Reciting the mission statement is a way of reminding board members of why they are there, and what the college is all about. That's important at a time when some Christian institutions have conflicted their missions or have experienced mission drift.

"It keeps us focused on the main thing," Ciccone said. "It keeps us focused on Christ. It keeps us focused on the support of Alaska Native students. It keeps us focused on what we're about as an academic institution."

Former Board Chair Paul Hawkinson was first approached about joining the board in 2014, not long after he became chief financial officer for the Covenant, a role he held until 2019. Hawkinson joined, in part, because he had long had an interest in the Covenant's work in Alaska, though he'd never had the chance to spend time there, and because the college could use board members with his kind of expertise in finance.

From the moment he arrived in Alaska, he was hooked. During his first visit, he was able to stop in Anchorage to reconnect with Covenant friends there and then drove to the campus in Soldotna, where he was struck by the beauty of the Alaskan landscape. Meeting the students, he said, was a transformative experience.

"I had the privilege of meeting some of the students in my first few minutes of being there," he said in a 2024 interview. "That set up a journey of hearing these incredibly redeeming stories of the importance of ACC at the center of many of these lives that have been difficult. I was overwhelmed by the beauty of the people and the work of ACC in their lives."

That kind of life transformation and redemption remains in the college's mission, said Hawkinson. He sees that mission as being "God's light and life, and encouragement and opportunity for Alaska Native students"—being a place where students can experience healing and grow in their faith and then go out and share the light and love in the world after they graduate. Since leaving his role with the Covenant denomination, Hawkinson has become a professor at North Park University, where he's run into ACC graduates and has seen how the college's ministry connects to the broader Covenant world.

Hawkinson said that nonprofit boards do their business in a variety of different ways. Some focus on fundraising, while others are more on what is called a "working board." The ACC board falls into a third category, with much of the work done on the committee level on policy only.

As a college professor, said Hawkinson, one of his real joys has been seeing the college expand the number of programs it offers, which he said has been especially impressive for such a small school. He said that the college also has a strong record of providing support for students, both academically and through counseling. He said that the college often provides a place for students to take the first steps on a larger journey of faith.

"What we're doing is being faithful to begin a journey of discipleship that will, hopefully, continue for a long time," he said. "It's a community that they can stay connected to. We're mindful that we're just part of launching a longer story."

That focus on discipleship, and setting students up for long-term faithfulness, was engrained in the college from the beginning, said Trevor Simpson, who served as the board chair in the college's early years. And it remains essential.

"I was there at the very beginning," said Simpson in an interview. "And I believe it still is completely the same mission and vision that they have now."

In the early years, the board was filled with people who had a passion for the school's mission and were willing to do whatever needed to be done to get the college off the ground. That commitment to the mission was still needed, but as the college grew, so did the need to find more board members and leaders with a wider range of skills to meet the challenges the school faced.

"I felt like the board needed to move from being a bunch of individuals that loved each other, Jesus, Keith, and this mission, but they needed to be more strategic and thoughtful and more deliberately placed," said Simpson. That's happened over the years, he said. But the mission of the school has remained the same.

Around 2006, the board recognized the need to provide expert support for Hamilton outside of board meetings. That led them to establish the President's Advisory Council (PAC), often made up of business leaders, donors, and others with expertise in organizational leadership. The group has no governing authority over the college but instead exists to help the college accomplish its mission.

The idea of an advisory council came out of a meeting Hamilton had with Douglas Ideker, a longtime friend and supporter of the college, and John Scott, another longtime friend. Ideker and Scott had begun meeting with Hamilton on an unofficial basis from the very beginning, and was part of a group of supporters from Arvada Covenant Church in Colorado, where Hamilton had been a youth pastor before becoming president of the college. Hamilton was Ideker's two boys' youth pastor and a special bond grew. Hamilton remembers sitting in his living room in Soldotna with Ideker and Scott, along with their wives, when Ideker introduced this council concept to Hamilton. Without question, Hamilton emphatically agreed that this was another crucial step in the leadership of ACC that was needed.

"They are here to support me and give advice," said Hamilton, in describing the role of the PAC, noting the PAC is not a decision-making body.

Every year Hamilton will pick two or three areas, often long-term projects, and will seek out the PAC's advice on how the projects might proceed. Part of the PAC's role is to think about the logistics of such projects and the wisdom of pursuing them, so that the ideas behind the projects are fully formed before they get to the board. The PAC, said Hamilton, often has the time and expertise to focus on those projects in a way that board members don't.

"They're retired business people, attorneys, professionals, and contractors that know the business. And they are great advisors to me," said Hamilton.

Advisory council members are also often generous supporters of the board—and will stand behind projects. PAC members, for example, were major donors to the college's VISION 2020 project, the athletic project, the Finish and Flourish campaign launched in 2024, and other long-term initiatives. Those PAC members meet by Zoom a few times a year, then gather once a year on campus overnight where they meet with Hamilton face to face as well as visit with students and senior staff to get a feel for what life at the college is like.

Hamilton also noted that even before the college was established, he began to meet with Doug Ideker (future PAC chair), George Mueller (future trustee, now passed), Trevor Simpson, Bob White, Sean Cherry, and Chris Anderson (future PAC) at Chili Peppers Mexican restaurant overlooking Mile High Stadium in

Denver. Their conversation was to dream about what ACC could be if the right plans fell into place. This was really the first unofficial advisory council for Hamilton, even as the first plans to purchase the property at 35109 Royal Place was in consideration. Hamilton has sought their support and advice ever since.

On an internal level, the college has gone through a series of structural evolutions. In the early days, everyone pitched in and there was little difference between the school's top leaders and the rest of the staff. Most staff had both academic and administrative roles and did whatever needed to be done. Hamilton was known to be seen riding the lawn mower on campus, Sean pushing snow, Jeff painting, etc. It has always been an all-out effort to get done what needed to get done.

"We just had 12 of us that started on July 1 of 2000 and there's nothing like it," Hamilton said.

As they moved towards accreditation, staff members began to be assigned new titles, such as Director of Enrollment, Director of Academics, Director of Development, some eventually becoming vice presidents. Much of the college's structure was shaped by watching what other similar ABHE colleges were doing and learning from their examples.

Eventually, the college grew enough to have an executive leadership team, the President's Cabinet, to share responsibility for running the college. That transition allowed college leaders to make decisions about policies and programs without having to involve the entire staff. For example, said Hamilton, leaders in student life made a decision about student curfews on their own and then reported to the other leaders, rather than having to get approval from everyone about those day-to-day details.

Hamilton said that the growth of the board has been a great asset to his role as president, and has been one reason why he's been able to sustain his leadership at the college for 25 years.

"I feel like I am never alone," he said.

That's a big change from the early years when he often felt the weight of leading the college and often felt he was making decisions on his own. Those days were lonely, he said in a 2025 interview.

"It probably took 10 years to turn the corner to where I felt like I had a board that was a partner in the leadership of the school, instead of me leading and asking the board to get answers to different things," he said. Now, Hamilton said, he has a range of experts, board members, advisors, and staff to depend on. Every group since the beginning has had significant impact on the present and future of the college.

In recent years, the board has developed a succession plan, for the day when Hamilton is no longer president. That plan also includes having what is known as "Key Personnel" insurance, in case something unexpected were to happen to Hamilton and he could no longer serve the college due to medical changes or death. Hamilton joked that he has to sleep at night with one eye open.

The plan also outlines how the college would go about hiring an interim president as well as how the search process for a new president would begin.

"Whenever in the future, when there is a transition, it will be managed by the board," said Hamilton. "Everybody knows their roles and what's going to happen, so it won't be a mystery."

One of the keys to the school's success has been retaining close ties to the Evangelical Covenant denomination and setting up processes to ensure that there's a mission fit between the staff and the college. "Trust and an alignment in beliefs remain essential," said Hamilton. These days when new staff or faculty are hired, the final step is a mission-fit meeting with Hamilton, either in person or online. This has helped tremendously to keep the staff speaking the same language and teaching the same core values that ACC has had since its beginning.

Even after staff are hired, there's a focus on getting the foundation right for staff. That foundation includes a sense of loyalty to the school's mission and success and a commitment to the students.

"They have to show that they are here for the missional purpose and not just for a paycheck," he said.

11

From the beginning, the goal of Alaska Christian College has been to create a supportive Christian community where students can grow in their faith, as well as develop the academic and personal skills they'll need as they grow further into adulthood. That Christian nurturing can happen in the classroom, as students study the Bible and the practical aspects of Christian ministry, as well as learn to apply their faith to the world around them. But much of it happens in the day-to-day life of the college, over meals in the dining room, during chapel services and Bible studies, and in the friendships students form while living together in a community with other Christians. It is more caught than taught in most circumstances.

However, not all students who apply for ACC are on the Christian journey...yet. When Hamilton was once asked about how many students who come are followers of Jesus, he made a very low number as his response. Why? He stated that ACC is an open enrollment college, like its predecessor North Park University, and all who meet the minimum academic qualifications are encouraged to apply.

As stated earlier, once accepted, no one is turned away their first year because of inability to pay nor because they are not Jesus followers, Christians. Over time, fewer students who write of their faith experience on their applications are Christians.

Many might have raised their hands at camp or will state that their family is of a certain denomination or church, but few understand what it means to follow Jesus daily when they come to ACC. The college has enrolled atheists, "nones," and those from a much different tradition from the evangelical roots of ACC and the Covenant church denomination. You might ask a student about their faith and their answer is, "Oh, I'm Catholic, Russian Orthodox, or Covenant." When asked what that means to them, few know their rationale or reason behind their answer. This is what ACC was created for, to bring any student, with any background, to join other students and also the staff, on the ride of their lifetime in a very caring and loving community. Many students, even those who were dismissed, will state that the one thing that they took away from ACC is that they knew that God loved them and so did the staff, extremely well.

Love for neighbor propels ACC to reach every student with the Good News of Jesus Christ, to disciple/mentor them, educate them in a field useful for their homes and communities, and see them receive healing from their past wounds, hurts, and addictions. It is a compelling Christian community, as Field Director Paul Wilson called it. Even today, at 25 years, it is ACC's clear call to meet a student no matter where they are at spiritually, emotionally, socially, and academically. With this mission call at the forefront, the student life scenario has always been difficult while satisfying, grieving while hopeful, and painful while healing. Empowering students and their spiritual life is the center of what ACC does.

The Student Services Department at ACC has long been the heart of the student experience—deeply committed to fostering a culture of care, connection, and growth. In a setting where many students arrive without personal vehicles, and often without prior exposure to Christian faith, the department stepped in to meet both practical and spiritual needs with intentionality and compassion.

At its core, Student Services prioritizes relationships. From early morning coffee meetups to late-night conversations in the residence halls, staff make it their mission to walk alongside students. Meals are shared not just to feed bodies, but to build trust and form community. Whether it is grabbing lunch in town, sitting down over hot chocolate, or cooking together in the residence halls, staff understand that relationships grow around the table.

For many students, particularly those from rural villages, the transition to campus life could feel overwhelming. Again, few came with church backgrounds, and many were unfamiliar with the hope and love of Christ. The Student Services team saw this as sacred ground. Discipleship wasn't limited to formal gatherings; it happened in quiet conversations, weekend trips, and service projects. Through these shared experiences, the seeds of faith were often planted and nurtured.

Recognizing the need for leadership development, especially for those returning home to serve in their communities, Student Services created opportunities for growth. Students were invited to serve as resident advisors, join the Student Appointed Leadership Team, and later, even become Student Services Interns. These roles gave them firsthand experience in leading peers, managing conflict, and planning community-wide events.

The team didn't just focus on spiritual and emotional growth, they met physical needs also. With most students lacking transportation, Student Services organized regular outings: trips to Homer, hikes through the Kenai wilderness, a day at the local pool, and city league basketball games. They also built and maintained an on-campus ice rink and operated a student-run store stocked with snacks, all small comforts that made a big difference in daily life.

Throughout the year, Student Services carried the responsibility of both support and accountability. They lived among students as dorm partners, navigated tough conversations when discipline was needed, and planned joyful moments like end-of-the-year retreats and campus celebrations.

They believed success wasn't just academic achievement—it was helping every student feel seen, supported, and deeply loved. Whether a student stayed one semester or graduated years later, the goal was always the same; that they would leave knowing Christ more fully and return home equipped to lead with courage, humility, and heart.

Discipline was always a tricky line to walk. While the love of Christ, mercy, and grace permeated the campus, it also meant requiring students to leave when they had to because of harm to themselves or others. ACC has a zero tolerance policy with any form of violence and providing alcohol to minors, and students must leave if in violation of this policy. Otherwise, over the years, the opportunities to stay amidst disciplinary issues was always possible if the student wanted to change and become a part of the campus with following important life covenants that are made with students needing care. Not always the case, but the three-strike policy works to allow the student three opportunities to correct themselves while seeking help from the counseling center (or mandated to do so) or making course corrections with the mentorship of a staff person. Every effort is provided for a student's successful retention to continue their pursuit of all what ACC's mission has to offer.

In recent years, much of the student life experience has evolved as cell phones have taken over the entertainment and time consumption of students. Without a doubt, the lack of engagement of a student, whether it is in their academics or student/spiritual life experience, is impacted by their use of their phones. COVID-19 made that clear when students spent nearly a year or longer separated from each other and relied on devices for their enjoyment and socialization. It has impacted the culture of ACC and other institutions. Student life staff, more than any other staff members on campus, have the pleasure, and difficulty, of front-lines ministry to students. ACC has had phenomenal leaders in this area where the rubber really meets the road in terms of impacting students' lives. ACC needs to continue to find ways to engage students, even with their phones in hand.

Thus, much of the responsibility for shaping the current Christian culture at the college is held by the student services staff, especially those who work in residence life. Their job, a residence life director said in an early 2025 interview, is to create an environment where students can grow ultimately in their spiritual life.

"We want to offer an opportunity for students to have a Christian education but more importantly to be discipled as Christians, and to learn about God, develop a relationship with God, and to learn how you are equipped as a child of God to serve the Church in the world," said one residence director.

There are some challenges in that students come from a diverse variety of backgrounds and experiences of faith. Again, there are students from Covenant churches, Catholic and Orthodox communities, Quaker and Moravian, and nondenominational settings. Some were baptized as babies and went to church a few times a year with their families, others served as altar boys in liturgical churches or went to church every week with their families.

"There's a real wide spectrum," said a residence life director. "Some students went to Bible camp and participated in their youth group and are stronger in their faith. Others are here and have no concept of who God is or what Jesus has done for salvation or redemption."

The students are also often away from home for the first time as young adults and have the chance to decide for themselves what faith means to them. Like most Christians, their investment in faith can vary from month to month, and even from day to day. Most of the students have some interest in growing as Christians, otherwise, they would not have chosen to come to a Christian college. But they often still experience discipleship in fits and starts.

Residence staff often provide a supporting role, tending to the physical, emotional, and social needs of students. That can range from organizing games in the student lounges and leading Bible studies to dealing with maintenance requests and roommate conflicts.

They also play a key role in connecting students to resources, like counseling, tutoring, and 12-step groups like Celebrate Recovery and serve as spiritual mentors. The staff also includes an assistant resident director (ARD) who lives in the halls with students, serving as a role model and keeping an eye on the community. That kind of presence in the lives of students matters.

"Our department also pursues students individually, to just get to know them and build trust and build relationships, talk to them, lead them to Christ and point them to Christ," a director said. "As often as you can pray with them, and pray *for* them."

The staff also provides organized activities for students so that spirituality is woven through the life of the college, with Tuesday night Bible studies, Thursday night small groups, volunteer mission trips, and chapels, where professors and staff often serve as speakers and other events. The fall semester often starts with a retreat called "Ignite," with usually a local pastor as a guest speaker, and a guest band, many years from Creekside Church in Elk Grove, California, and led by Peter Neumann. The spring semester, when new students arrive, the entire campus also spends one day on the "Re-Ignite" retreat, to recapture some of the spiritual energy from the beginning of the year and to remind students of all they had learned so far.

Elizabeth (Lizzy) Bieber, another student services director at ACC, said it's important for students to experience a supportive environment at school, where they are loved and cared for and have access to the resources needed to deal with some of the challenges of their past. Many of the students have dealt with loss and grief, along with issues like substance abuse and other forms of abuse that are part of the reality of life in rural Alaska.

"Even if they haven't come to faith in the time that they're here, it's important that they leave feeling loved, that they leave knowing that they have a safe place, that they have people who have modeled good relationships and trust and care for them," said Bieber, who has also been on staff since 2021. "The goal is to let them encounter the Lord and have the Holy Spirit move in their life. But I think beyond that, too, that they come here and see what it is to be loved, cared for, and safe. And I think that's part of it too."

The Student Services staff also organize the social life of the campus, as well as communicating with the students about everything from mealtimes and rides, to church, to organized errand runs into Soldotna where students can pile into a van and go to town to get their shopping done. The staff also sets up other off-campus outings to events like the Native Youth Olympics, a sporting competition that showcases traditional athletic contests, Native Musicale, CYAK young adult retreats, and mission trips.

"We do a lot of fun activities, whether that's campfires, or trips to the beach, or hiking trips, or ice skating, or sledding, or ice fishing, or day trips to Homer, Seward, or Whittier," said Bieber.

The weekly schedule is displayed on the campus digital bulletin board, emailed to students, and posted to a Facebook group for the campus community. That Facebook group became a lifeline during COVID-19, but has become less effective as the pandemic faded and students had to learn how to navigate life together with a new normal, where things were not exactly the way they had been before.

Along with the resident directors who live among the students, the school has a staffer for the front desk at night who keeps the door locked and the students safe, while also being a visible staff presence in the building, which can be helpful in a community of young adults. Keeping students safe also can mean enforcing the college's rules, which are designed to promote a healthy and respectful community.

"The heart of our department is to have a Christ-like community here, to treat one another with respect and do things that are safe and healthy for yourself and honoring God," a Student Services staff member stated. "So our student handbook outlines a lot of different policies about showing respect to others and how you talk and how you dress and what you watch, what you listen to. Then regarding substances, we have a no substance policy on campus regarding drugs and alcohol, and tobacco is limited to a designated space on campus."

Part of the balancing act for staff is setting boundaries and enforcing the college's policies while helping students grow and develop, rather than punishing them for their mistakes. That can involve putting in place a "student action plan" for support services that can help a student grow and mature. The point, said Bieber, is to help the students find the support system they need to stay on campus and succeed.

"We will put into place an action plan where they're going to have three counseling sessions, and then find two other avenues of long-term support," said Bieber. That can involve attending spiritual life events or finding a staffer who can be a mentor and spend time with the students to help them with their struggles. Patience is a key to helping students succeed.

> The leap in faith to move to and work at Alaska Christian College from Arizona was a momentous one in my life and walk with Christ. Working with other believers with one common mission has been the best experience of my life so far. I've really seen how God moves here at Alaska Christian College. As part of the Spiritual Life team here at ACC, God has grown and shaped me a lot. Getting to know and grow alongside fellow staff and building meaningful relationships with our students has been a beautiful experience for me. I am extremely blessed to be a part of what God is doing at Alaska Christian College.
>
> — Angelo Cickavage

The Student Services staff aren't the only people invested in helping students grow and feel cared for. Instead, that's the responsibility of all the staff, even those who don't work directly with students. That's something Dan Franklin, the college's recent volunteer facilities manager, said he learned while serving as a volunteer, doing maintenance work at the college for the past five years. In an interview, he recalled an encounter he'd had with a student early on during his time as a volunteer. Franklin said he walked through the basement of a dorm and saw a student there, lying on a couch, and skipping class. The student, Franklin recalled, had been going through a hard time and instead of getting help or going to class, was hiding out.

That angered Franklin. He thought about all the volunteers and donors who'd give their time, talents, and resources to make the college's ministry possible. Yet here was a student, he thought, who was throwing it all away. Then, while walking across the parking lot after leaving the hall, Franklin began to remember all the mistakes he'd made in his life, all the times he'd failed to be the person he wanted to be or wasted time and opportunities he'd been given. It was as if God was reminding him of his failings and all the grace he had received over his lifetime. At that moment, Franklin said, his job was not to judge the student or look down on them but to love, support, and pray for him.

Later in the day, Franklin said the student came to him and embraced him. Franklin was confused and asked the student what was going on. The student said he'd seen Franklin, and in that moment, had felt God's presence. He got off the couch and went to talk to a counselor, asking for help. That encounter led to a friendship with Franklin and set the student on a path that transformed his life.

The change didn't happen right away. Franklin recalled that after the student had graduated, he called one night to talk to Franklin about his struggles and how he wanted to give up and was thinking about ending his life. What was the point, after all, he wondered. But having someone to talk to, someone he had a long and committed friendship with, helped the student keep going. That student now is married, has several kids and a steady career, and is doing well.

"I learned it's not my job to judge people," Franklin said, recalling that encounter. "My job is to pray for them and love them unconditionally and let God do the work."

Now, whenever he walks across the parking lot of the college, Franklin said he feels like he's walking on holy ground, knowing that God is at work in the lives of students and that he and other staffers and the students are all part of a larger story of God making the world right.

Some students need more support than the college can provide on its own, especially when it comes to issues of substance abuse, a longstanding issue in Native communities. Sometimes those students have to leave to get treatment before they can continue their studies—though, in at least one case, a student was able to do both. In an interview, a student services staff member said that at least one student was able to attend classes while living at Freedom House, a Christian recovery program not far from the school. That student successfully graduated from both the Freedom House program and ACC in 2025. A MIRACLE! The school staff also helps students make arrangements to attend Alcoholics Anonymous, Celebrate Recovery, and other 12-Step groups.

Hamilton recounts one story that forever changed his view of evil. While at home in bed one night, he got a disturbing call from Sean Hoffbeck who was serving in student services at the time. Sean excitedly asked Hamilton to immediately come over to the college. A student was "flipped out." Hamilton raced to the college to find one of the female students angrily tossing the foyer to the dining hall of all its tables, chairs, and hanging plants. Sean had also called the Alaska State Troopers as he wasn't sure what was all happening. When Hamilton looked into the eyes of the student, who was growling and speaking unintelligible words, he knew what it was. Seminary never prepares you for this and it is hard to describe until you see it face to face. This student was under attack by a demon and was clearly possessed. Hoffbeck, along with other student services staff, were praying and quoting Scripture as Hamilton was doing, all to no avail. In fact, the shrieking got worse the more they prayed and quoted Scripture.

The student got away from them and headed down the stairs to the bottom of the Quyana Residence Hall where the entrance door was locked so the student was "trapped" at the bottom of the stairs. Everyone could hear the yelling, the pounding on the door downstairs, and the torment. Hamilton, unsure of what else to do, grabbed a Covenant hymnal nearby. Why? One of the classes on mission and evangelism in the early days was taught by Rev. Gordon and Geneva Christensen of the Congo, Africa. They had written an amazing book named *Fire in Their Bones* and Hamilton and the students had read it for class. He remembered a story in the book of the Christensen's casting out a demon, after three days of trying, by singing the Easter hymn, "Low in the Grave He Lay."

All of the student services staff and Hamilton began to sing as the demon screamed louder than before, but during the chorus of "Up from the grave He arose" the second time through, it got silent downstairs. Hamilton ran down there to find the student lying on the ground, clothes torn, and semi-conscious. He asked if "they" were okay. No response. He asked their name. No response. He asked which village they were from, and "Hooper" was the first response, which was correct. Hamilton began to see the student start to tense up again, make fists, and eyes began narrowing while breathing erratically. He told the student to repeat after him a prayer of deliverance and salvation, which the student did until, all of a sudden, the student went limp again. This time, the student looked right at Hamilton and asked, "Keith, what are you doing down here? What am I doing down here? Why are my clothes torn and my head hurt?" The student had been banging their head against the locked door and tearing their clothes. Hamilton tenderly told the student that they were safe and if there was anything he could do to help. By the way, the Alaska state trooper had arrived and witnessed this entire last exchange and, when he realized it was a spiritual matter, quickly left the stairway, and was clearly confused about what he had just seen!

The student then asked Hamilton what was going on and he explained about the exorcism. The student was incredulous, asking, "How can this be?" Hamilton asked if they had ever opened the door to evil things in their life and it was discovered that the student, like many in their village, "played the game" Ouija Board. Hamilton explained that this could have been the gateway to Satan's power in their life. The student exclaimed it was just a game by Parker Brothers! Hamilton disagreed, it was a gateway into the darkness outside of life with Christ. The student gathered themself and returned to their room, under the care of the student services staff. Later, the name of the demon was pronounced in a time of healing prayer, "Mayhem." You see, since the age of three when this child of God was sexually abused, their life had been mayhem. The student said this was the first time in their life that voices were not in their head telling them what to do. This student was not only freed from the Evil One, but the student ended up finishing the year and working on the summer staff over the summer, a new creation in Christ Jesus. While Hamilton recalls three experiences with exorcisms in his time at ACC, this one demonstrated the most vicious attack on a student and the most rewarding ending. A MIRACLE! Sometimes, Debbie Hamilton has wondered with any of her clients at New Hope Counseling Center whether mental issues are simply behavioral health and which are spiritual. ACC staff are fighting a battle for the very lives of their students at times, praying in the name of Jesus for complete freedom from the bondage they may carry, and knowing that "greater is He that is in you, than he that is in the world."

Hamilton also fondly recalls the many mission trips he has personally led to Ensenada and Mexicali, Mexico, with students and staff from ACC. For 35 years, including his two youth pastorates, he has traveled with groups to serve on the ground in Mexico, just across the border. Once a Covenant short-term missionary to Mexico in 1984–85, his love for the Mexican people has always been a big part of his life and ministry. Each spring, he would take as few as five, and in 2025 he took the largest team of 18 south of the border to serve alongside long-term friends who used to run the program sponsored by Azusa Pacific University. The students would do Vacation Bible School–type programs, youth group nights, church services, painting, cleaning, light construction, serve at mental health facilities, at-risk children centers, pick-up games in the park, and even once cleaned out an old brothel!

The experiences have been life-changing for ACC students that may have never even left the state and who have traveled to a foreign third-world country to serve Jesus. Many decisions for Christ have been made and many students have increased their heart for mission. Thanks to generous donors and churches like Rock Harbor Covenant Church in Rocklin, California, funds have been raised each year to assist the students to make the trek, even while using standby or mileage seat tickets. Not only is it rewarding for the students and staff who take the week off of college, but they also get credit toward their 10 hours per semester of Christian Service that is required before a student can graduate from ACC. In order for a student to go, they must also carry a 3.0 grade point average, as they will miss classes for the week. Hamilton believes that service/mission trips to rural Alaska are also very effective, but there is something entirely different happening to students when they see poverty and faith collide in Mexico, something you can't teach in a textbook. Hamilton estimates that approximately 75 of the 900 plus students who have attended ACC have been to the mission field in Mexico. Fantastico!

Staffers on campus who work directly in student services also collaborate with the counselors at New Life Counseling Center, reminding students that going to counseling is not a sign of weakness, but instead is a resource that can help them succeed. Admitting to mental illness or emotional struggles still has a stigma attached to it, and many of the students are used to dealing with their challenges on their own. Each ACC staff and faculty member, regardless of their role, receives a number of free counseling opportunities at NHCC. Student services staff, however, have unlimited visits, as is needed, to seek counsel from the wise leaders at NHCC.

When students leave campus, whether they have graduated or had to leave or for some other reason, the college keeps an open door, when possible, for their return.

"We tell them we are family," said Bieber. "You are welcome back anytime."

Some students also end up staying around after graduation as interns, through a program funded by the Murdock Charitable Trust, some eventually also join the staff. Alumni also come back to the school at times to speak to students. Some students stay around during the summer break to serve as Summer Ambassadors for the college, working alongside summer volunteers and talking with visitors, primarily Sowers team members, about their experience at the college.

John Henry Jr., a Native American Apache student from Arizona, said that the supportive community at the college, where students can work on their academic skills while being able to access counseling and support groups, had been amazing. Henry, who was in his mid-20s when he arrived on campus, said he needed that mix of support to deal with some of the challenges he faced as a young adult.

During an interview on a group outing for students during graduation week, as the college community went on a Kenai Fjords boat trip in Seward as part of the end-of-year's festivities, Henry talked about some struggles he'd had growing up, where substance abuse and family instability made it hard to get a strong foundation for life. He'd heard about the college while attending a conference for Indigenous young people, and decided it might be just what he needed. While at the college, he'd received tutoring to brush up on his academics and counseling to help him work through past struggles. Just as importantly, Henry said, he had a good friend and developed a trusting relationship with the staff.

"Sometimes people just need someone who will listen," he said. "It's been a really helpful experience being here." John graduated from ACC in 2025 and currently is the Information Technology Intern for a year at ACC.

Kaylie Williams, a 2024 graduate, said that ACC helped her make the transition from living in a tight-knit small village of about 600 people to life at college. Williams, who hopes to go to nursing school, said that growing up she was shy and that being around strangers or crowds of people was difficult. That was especially true during COVID-19.

"I was kind of the girl who was in the back of the classroom and never wanted to be around people," she said. Coming to ACC, and eventually serving as a student ambassador, gave her more self-confidence and helped her grow in her faith, she said. The support of the staff and professors helped her trust others more as well. Williams said that being in a small college like ACC prepared her to move to a bigger school.

"I've seen myself grow closer with God and I don't feel like I'm alone," Williams said. "I feel like I can talk to anyone."

> Summer Sheldon is the first second-generation student to attend ACC. Her parents not only attended ACC, but they were also both recognized with the Alumni of the Year award in different years, Don Fancher and Sylvia Sheldon. Summer just completed her third semester and is majoring in General Studies. She also is the first female to join the marine engines class! She plans to continue her education after graduating from ACC. Summer grew up in Kiana and Kotzebue.

A number of students who come to ACC are isolated at first, in part because they are on their own for the first time and in part because they've come to rely on the tight-knit community at home and now need to learn how to make new friends. Although most of the students come from Native communities that are very similar, some come from small remote villages, while others come from communities that are on Alaska's road system, which are different experiences. One of the key jobs for staff is putting students at ease, especially in the early days of their college experience, and giving them time to start building the relational network that can lead to long-term success. While ACC is focused on Alaska Native students, many non-Native students from outside the state or local commuters have also participated widely in what ACC has to offer.

> Attending ACC has been an incredible journey for me. Not only have I furthered my education, but I've also deepened my

relationship with God. Throughout my time here, I've had the pleasure of meeting amazing people from diverse backgrounds, which has enriched my experience even more. As my graduation approaches, I can't help but reflect on how transformative this period has been for my personal and professional growth. The knowledge and connections I've gained will undoubtedly shape my future in profound ways. I hope others will also find their path to success and fulfillment through education, just as I have at ACC

— Kenzie

Allysia Smith, a 2017 graduate and member of the Navajo tribe, spoke to graduates at the spring of 2024 Commencement Banquet, during a dinner honoring the students and their families. Smith told the graduates that when she first arrived on campus, she was anxious and withdrawn, not sure of where she fit in.

"I had built up a resentment toward people," Smith said, adding that her resentment served as a kind of safety barrier to keep people away. But the school became a place where she felt safe and could learn to trust others and be part of a community. Before she graduated, she became anxious again, as she had no idea where her life was heading next.

Then she learned about an opportunity to work with children at a ministry in Oaxaca, Mexico, serving under the leader that was formerly from Hamilton's youth group in Colorado. That experience changed her life forever and made her want to serve other people. "I had seen the same love that existed at ACC in the people of Oaxaca, and it was contagious, and I wanted to stay there," she said.

After nine months in Mexico, she came home with hopes of getting involved in a ministry to Native communities in the United States and eventually joined the staff of a ministry in a community called Little Earth, in South Minneapolis, where most of the residents come from Indigenous backgrounds. Leaving Oaxaca had been difficult, she said, but Smith said that she'd felt a call to help her own community and people thrive. Still, the road to ministry wasn't always easy.

"It wasn't all glitter and sunshine when I got home," Smith told students, who were seated around tables in the college's dining hall, surrounded by family and friends. Smith told them about some of the challenges she'd faced in ministry and how it took time for her to find her way. But the lessons she learned at ACC and the faith that had grown in the time at the college, helped see her through these challenges.

She encouraged students to rely on their faith and to seek out ways to put their faith to work to serve and love those around them.

"I encourage you to think of the steps you've already taken," she told them. "There is strength in your story. It won't be easy, but if you choose to live a life for God, your cup will always overflow." Allysia was voted on by the Board of Trustees to be the 2024 Alumna of the Year, based on her emulation of the mission of ACC throughout her life since graduation. The Alum of the Year Award is annually voted on by the board and was initiated by Rev. Nathan Toots, in 2007, when he was chair of the Board of Trustees.

> I was a student from 2013 to 2016 and was working toward an A.A. Degree in Christian Ministry. My time at ACC was great and I gained a lot of knowledge in so many ways. What really benefited me during my time at ACC was being able to learn so much from Amanda Hoekstra about financial needs as well as being able to be more independent. I learned about the great history of churches in Alaska and the differences and similarities between denominations. A lot of people there had a huge impact on my life. I cannot be grateful enough or put into words how thankful I am.
>
> — Cora Foster Strong

> I went to ACC in 2004 and did the two-year biblical studies program. This was before the associate programs they have now. I lived on campus for four years. I appreciated being able to live on campus while I worked on a degree at KPC next door. I met my husband at ACC and we even got married on campus in the PCC. I desperately needed New Hope when I was a student and I am so thankful that those services were available to us. My husband and I have two children. I teach fourth and fifth grade ELA and math. We miss ACC a lot!

— Sylvia Tuckfield Andrew

I am from Kwigillingok, Alaska. While at ACC I learned that being a follower of Jesus means letting Christ shape who I am; discipleship has always been the key at ACC. In addition to growing in my relationship with Christ, I developed helpful study skills that equipped me to continue on and earn my Bachelor's and Master's in Education. Returning to rural Alaska has been a dream of mine.

Today I am an elementary math teacher and basketball coach in the small village of Tuntululiak. Leaving my village to go to ACC was a big step for me in so many ways; a much bigger town, meeting and living with new people, different foods, a lot of homework, so many trees, and no gym to play basketball. Many ACC students come from rural villages where basketball is a huge focus and unfortunately, the gym nearest to ACC was about ten miles away.

— Jimmy Andrew

12

The college's annual summer volunteer building season, often referred to by Hamilton and other college leaders as the Sowers program, was born out of necessity. It also became essentially an ongoing campaign that was responsible for most of the building projects in the school's history. During the college's first year of operation, everyone lived in one building, which was unsustainable.

"We just knew we needed to get the guys out of the main house," said Hamilton.

Doing that meant building three cabins on the school's grounds. In the summer of 2001, five volunteer teams from Covenant churches made their way to Soldotna to work on the cabins. While the volunteers got a great deal done, by the end of the summer there was still more to be done around campus.

"And of course, some of them said, 'Hey can we come back next summer?'" said Hamilton. "And we said, 'Sure. We'd love to have you.'"

Those first cabins were finished in November 2001, with help from Bob Bode, a member of Arvada Covenant, who helped provide some of the funds needed for the project along with the North Mankato Covenant Church. Hamilton and other leaders began looking for other projects that volunteers could work on, like converting the main house's double garage into the college's first dining hall.

Why Sowers? It is a reference to the idea of farmers sowing seeds from the Bible. The name had been first suggested by Jon Taylor, a college staff member and alum who worked in advancement. For every summer since its inception, ACC has been gifted with thousands of volunteers providing tens of thousands of dollars in donated sweat equity, saving the college hundreds of thousands and millions of dollars. A MIRACLE!

Along with providing volunteer leaders, summer church groups also brought an infusion of resources to the college in its early years, and became the driving force for a series of capital campaigns. The first campaign was known as Anchoring Our Future and was focused on providing funding for the first residence hall and dining hall, both of which were needed as the school moved toward accreditation.

From the very beginning, the college began asking volunteers to bring a gift of $500 per person to pay for the materials needed for various construction projects. Those funds helped jumpstart those projects, providing a ready supply of cash and ensuring that a lack of resources would not slow volunteers down. The staff would also spend months planning to make the best use of volunteers.

"We put together lists all year long of things that needed to get done that could wait until the summer teams got here," said Hamilton. "And when the summers got here, we would start going through those lists one by one and try to match up people with their skills and with the jobs we needed to get done."

It took a while for the college to learn how to best use volunteers. There were a few missteps, like the time a volunteer group put up a wall in the wrong location, and by the time the staff supervising the project realized what was happening, it was done. The next week, a group of volunteers had to come in quietly and take down the wall and put a new one up in the right place.

"Sometimes those jobs didn't always go perfectly," said Hamilton.

Along with putting up the frames for walls and hanging drywall, volunteers also lent a hand with other projects, such as sewing curtains for the new residence halls or planting and maintaining gardens to beautify the campus. Some of the volunteers, under the direction of longtime Native college staff member Mary Hunt, learned how to make "kuspuks" in those early years, a traditional Native garment, for the students to wear at college programs and to sell at various auctions the college did.

Over the years, the volunteers became a wonderful asset for the college, providing much-needed funds and volunteers but also building a network of support for the college, whose love for ACC endured long after they returned home. ACC didn't have or need a maintenance project fund because the team members provided generously for all the year-round projects, most of them being completed in the summer.

Currently, due to the rising cost of hosting volunteers, gas, food, insurance, and all the other necessities, volunteers are asked to pay $400 for room and board and in-state transportation for the week and another $550 (up only $50 in 25 years) for building materials. Those funds mean that volunteers can have warm meals and a comfortable place to stay, without having to cook for themselves or sleep in tents. That's helpful, said Hamilton, as many of the college's volunteers are older church members who are often retired. They very much appreciate this opportunity as no passports, stairs, rental vehicles, hotel rooms, or foreign languages are needed at ACC for them to serve.

Hamilton recalled the story of Dan Lewis, in his late 80s at the time, from Arvada Covenant in Colorado. Lewis was a retired master electrician, who showed up during a summer when the finishing touches were being put on one of the college residence halls. That included installing light switches and covers for all the electrical outlets in the building. While Lewis had trouble walking, his mind and skills were still sharp. College leaders arranged for him to have a comfortable chair that he could move from switch to switch, outlet to outlet, and he was able to spend the entire week finishing that project. It had to be done by someone, why not 80-something-year-old Dan? He was awarded the ACC "Ten-ure" award based on the idea of college "tenure." Any volunteer who spends 10 years serving at ACC receives this award during one of the lunches while they are back serving on campus. For Dan, Hamilton was able to do it in front of the entire Arvada Covenant congregation, a wonderful moment for all.

"There's a job for everyone," said Hamilton. Hamilton is also known for telling summer volunteers they only need to work during daylight hours when they come up to volunteer. Of course, this is a humorous reference to Alaska's very long summer days.

Some of the college's volunteers have turned their week at the college into an extended stay, with some volunteering for as much as a month or longer at a time, or combining the volunteering with a chance to do some tourist exploration of Alaska.

That led to the start of a new program called "Team Nehemiah," named for the book of the Bible that recounts how the walls of Jerusalem were rebuilt. Nehemiah volunteers help maintain the campus's buildings and work on new projects throughout the year outside of summer months. But they do more than build walls, said Hamilton.

"They're coming up here and spending time and hanging out with students and going to chapel, being part of student life," he said.

"They're also building the walls we don't have to move twice," added Sean Hoffbeck, the longtime vice president of operations for the college.

The Sowers program and Team Nehemiah members played an essential role in the construction of the college's newly constructed athletic center, a 28,000 square foot facility built for about $3.5 million including the paving of the parking lot. Having volunteers on the project cut the cost of the project drastically and made it affordable for the college. The original architect estimated the cost to build the AC and its attached buildings was $11 million. With the great support of so many volunteers, the actual cost was one-third of that amount! A MIRACLE! As previously noted, getting the AC built was complicated, in large part due to disruptions from the COVID-19 pandemic. The college began raising funds for the gym in 2019, and by 2020, much of the needed funding was in hand.

What the college did not have, however, was the materials during COVID-19. While waiting for materials, Sowers teams worked on every aspect of the new athletic center to keep the project moving.

"The money still kept coming, but we couldn't get steel," said Hamilton.

Yet even in the chaos of the pandemic, Hamilton saw signs that God was at work.

"When it was all said and done, we spent about three and a half million dollars on the first phase of the AC and we were able to keep it low because of these amazing volunteers who came up over the last five summers to help us build," Hamilton said.

Again, Dennis Schnicke, the volunteer who built the additional three classrooms and the Taikuu Residence Hall, was the key person for the construction of the AC. When Samaritan's Purse was negotiating to have him work for their project in the

Denali National Forest, Hamilton heard of his availability to serve in retirement and invited Dennis and his wife, Connie—who would later lead the food service department—to lunch to share the vision of the classroom building and new residence hall. Dennis, almost without hesitation, signed on board and spent the next seven years serving alongside his good friends Ike Dotomain and Larry Streiff to construct the largest project in ACC's history.

The college has now launched a new capital campaign called Finish and Flourish, where one-half of the $1.5 million for the campaign will go towards *Finish*, adding a much-needed lobby onto the front of the AC. The other half will financially help the college *Flourish* in the future, mainly by providing funds for recruitment, marketing, retention, academic programs, scholarships, and the Legacy Endowment.

"We're doing extra media. We're using a lot of funds to get the news out that Alaska Christian College is open statewide," said Hamilton. "We want your students."

The capital campaign will also help fund plans to expand the college's technical and vocational offers. In the fall of 2024, the college launched a pilot program with the Yamaha company to teach students how to work on outdoor motors through online modules and hands-on experience. That program will allow students to be certified to work on motors at Yamaha dealers as they progress through the various certificates in their training. The college is working on developing other career tech programs, possibly teaching students to drive heavy equipment and get their CDLs, among other options. The capital campaign will also allow the school to rehire some of the faculty it lost due to the post-COVID pandemic decline in students, which led to layoffs.

Simeon Paxman started the Career and Technical Education program at ACC by teaching an Introduction to Outboard Systems course in the fall of 2024. He noted that this program came together as the result of hard work and collaboration with groups such as the Alaska Maritime Education Consortium and State agencies, such as the Department of Labor and Workforce Development and the Alaska Department of Education and Early Development. Students who graduate from the Yamaha-developed courses will be able to work as technicians for Yamaha dealers nationwide.

Hamilton said that in the early years of the Sowers program, he first drew mostly on the connections he'd made during his time as a Covenant youth pastor. That led him to call friends who were leaders at places like Community Covenant Church in Shawnee, Kansas, Clairemont Covenant Church in San Diego, Arvada Covenant Church in Colorado, and Castle Oaks Covenant Church in Colorado.

"We were just scrambling," Hamilton recalled. "I just asked people, would you be willing to come up to Alaska?"

Hamilton said the college has also benefited from the Covenant's historical love of mission work in Alaska, which dates back to the 1800s. And then there is the appeal of traveling to Alaska, which is on so many people's bucket lists.

"It's Alaska, which is pretty cool," he said. "It's not Iowa."

To help current and graduated students learn leadership skills, connect with the broader Church, and allow them to see they had a part in building the college, the advancement staff started the summer Ambassadors program around 2010. As many as five students stay on campus for the summer, work alongside volunteers, share their stories with volunteers, and serve as hosts. Many Ambassadors have formed long-term friendships with the volunteers who visit during the summer, and the encouragement that students receive can keep students going, even when they hit hard times during the school year.

"They become lifelong friends," said Hamilton. "We will have students that have graduated, that will come back to campus a certain week in the summertime to see their friends from different churches. These volunteers, Sowers teams, from the lower 48, have poured into our students and have loved on them not just the week they are here, but afterwards as well."

The students also gain a sense of self-confidence while working with volunteers and learn that they have something important to offer to the ministry of their college.

Having volunteers on campus also is a reminder to staff and students alike of how many people had a role in building and sustaining the school. Hoffbeck said that sometimes people volunteer for mixed reasons—a sense of adventure, wanting to serve, and the chance to experience Alaska and do a little fishing. But they come back year after year because they fall in love with the school and its mission.

"We realize that the college doesn't belong just to us," said Hoffbeck. "It doesn't belong just to the students or the staff. This college belongs to people who are scattered all over the lower 48 because Alaska Christian College has become their college. That keeps them coming back."

Hamilton said that volunteers do go fishing and get a chance to enjoy the beauty of God's creation, but those experiences aren't what matter in the end.

"Yes, they get a fish, but it's no longer about the fishing," Hoffbeck said. "It's about walking around and saying, my fingerprints are all over this place. We joke sometimes that it's sleepover camp for senior citizens, but at the end of the day, this is a place where Jesus lives, and because Jesus lives here, people want to come."

The planning process for Sowers usually starts in August, not long after the last group of volunteers packs and departs. Hoffbeck and other staffers walk through the campus, taking stock of all that the volunteers accomplished and compiling a list of things that will need to be done in the future. They keep adding to the list throughout the school year and try to match projects to volunteer teams, with a myriad of expertise they know will be coming to the college in the future. Also at summer's end, Hamilton hosts a dinner event at a local restaurant to thank the myriad of volunteers and Ambassadors who stayed through the summer to bring it all together. The best time of the evening is when the evaluations are read aloud with comments about the Sowers' experiences and specific people they want to praise. It is a humbling and joyful experience to hear the stories from the summer and to see the aggregate score of their evaluations. At the end of the summer in 2023 and 2024, the 10-question evaluation, filled out by the Sowers teams, scored a whopping approximately 9.8 out of 10. This is amazing, but ACC has had 25 years to work on how best to serve those who serve ACC best.

The sign-up process for volunteers usually begins in October, with Hoffbeck working alongside Eric Johnson, the school's Vice President for Advancement, to communicate with volunteers. The college can accommodate about 45 volunteers per week, so there's some juggling to make all the groups fit. Once the groups are scheduled, the individual Sowers application includes a skills inventory, which gives ACC staff a sense of the kinds of abilities that volunteers have. Volunteers who work in the trades—plumbers, electricians, and carpenters—can be particularly helpful. The form also asks if volunteers have been on mission trips before or if they have other skills, like sewing, painting, or working on landscaping. Although the work is primarily focused on building or updating facilities, there is something for everyone to do once they arrive on campus.

"We have all these lists of volunteers coming, with an idea of what their skill set is, before they ever hit campus," said Hoffbeck.

Groups usually arrive on Saturday and then have a free day on Sunday to get acclimated and perhaps do a little sightseeing, such as taking a whale-watching cruise along the Kenai Fjords or a dogsled ride with mushing dogs. Then Monday morning, they are off to work, with tasks designed to match the group's skills. Sometimes a team will arrive with someone who has a surprising skill set, such as the time a professional roofer showed up with a church group right about the time one of the buildings was ready for roofing, with no leader.

"We put him on the roof and the volunteers were able to get a whole large-scale roof shingled in a week," said Hoffbeck. Hoffbeck also told about the need for carpet installation in a cabin remodel and a professional carpet installer was on the team that week. Another time a significant and unexpected plumbing issue developed in one of the college's buildings, and three professional plumbers were already on-site working, ready to switch to the new project. A MIRACLE!

> ACC needed an excavator to move gravel around on campus, especially for the construction of the AC. It was a significant investment of $57,000 and staff questioned whether it would be the best use of funds. However, about a month after the purchase, on the first day of school, the dormitory septic system and leach drain field failed. Due to the excavator being available, staff were able to respond immediately, digging a new leach field and making the necessary repairs without bringing in outside professionals. This not only resolved the issue quickly, it also saved the college a substantial amount of money, likely $20-30 thousand. In fact, the cost savings from doing the work in-house allowed the college to recoup a majority of the excavator's purchase price. What

originally seemed like a risky financial decision turned out to be another miracle on Royal Place. A MIRACLE!

Most of the groups are overseen by long-term volunteers like Dan Franklin, a retired firefighter who serves as one of the college's volunteer facilities leaders. Dan had volunteered for years during the summers while he was still working, and then he and his wife, Terri, sold their home and moved to Soldotna to be full-time volunteers.

"He sits down every Monday morning with the volunteers and shares with them," said Hoffbeck. "He tells them, 'I don't get paid to do this. I feel called to do this,' and people resonate with that."

Hamilton knows that the need for Sowers and Team Nehemiah's talented individuals will always be needed at ACC. With 27 different building or purchase projects over the 25 years, there is always something that will need maintenance attention. As the first buildings from 2000-2005 are beginning to show wear and tear, it will take many future summers full of willing volunteers to keep the campus looking "like-new," as Hamilton states is the goal for all they have. Every building and facility belongs to the Lord, and taking care of them is a top priority, as funds and laborers are provided. The volunteers are one of the pillars of ACC in every way.

For most of the college's history, many of the staff were considered missionaries, in that they had to raise the support needed to pay their salaries. Often the churches that supported staffers during the year were the same congregations that would send volunteers, giving the staff a chance to meet with them face-to-face and build friendships.

"This is not just a one-way relationship," said Hoffbeck. "The money is coming from one direction, but the care and community is coming from both sides. It has become a hallmark of what we do here." Hamilton adds, they have always attempted to make sure the road was two-way, when possible, for ACC to also bless the churches that have served ACC. One example is the Mission Hills Covenant Church in the Palm Springs, California, area, which has sent teams for many years in the summer and has also sent their pastor, Dr. Chris Hushaw, to serve as the Pastor in Residence. When they asked if ACC could send a team of students to work on their newly acquired, and badly-needing-remodeling, church facility, the answer was an emphatic yes! This is a two-way, reverse mission trip that 12 students thoroughly enjoyed. Having Chick-fil-A and In-N-Out Burger nearby seemed to help make the trip spectacular as well.

At times, there has been pushback about the summer volunteer programs at the college because having that many volunteers on campus takes up an enormous amount of time and energy. While the volunteers do a great deal of work and bring much-needed resources to campus, there have been concerns that running the summer volunteer program can distract from the school's bigger mission of educating and discipling Alaska Natives.

Those concerns are valid, says Hamilton. However, the college has continued to host volunteers in part because those volunteers make the mission possible. Their time, energy, and donations allowed the college to build the facilities needed to house, feed, and educate students, something that tuition dollars would not have been able to do.

Having volunteers on campus has also developed a widespread and deep network of highly motivated supporters who want to see the college succeed and who want to see young Alaskans thrive. And those volunteers keep giving after they have left campus and some have even remembered the college in their wills, allowing ACC to continue growing its endowment, which will help the college be sustainable over the long haul.

"There are a lot of ripple effects that happen from us dedicating 10 weeks of summer to these mission teams. We are grateful for every volunteer," said Hamilton.

ACC's skid-steer/Bobcat was aging and staff faced the reality that it needed to be replaced. It had been purchased by a family foundation for $17,000 as a used rental in 2003. Twenty years later, ACC sold it for $27,000! Staff spoke to President Hamilton about this need and he acknowledged there was not any extra money for the remaining $40,000 that was needed. Literally, about five minutes after that conversation, staff was called back to Keith's office to hear that the original donor offered to donate $25,000 more for the brand-new skid-steer! With $15,000 to go, Hamilton contacted life-long friends in Shoreline, Washington. The wife especially loved driving these skid-steers and they committed to cover all the rest of the cost, after Hoffbeck sold some of the attachments ACC no longer needed. A MIRACLE!

The volunteers also fill another need that the college consistently has. Many colleges rely on tuition and other fees to pay the bills and supplement with income from donations, largely from alumni, especially alums who have gone on to have financial success after graduation. That model does not work for ACC.

"Our alumni base can't give the money that most colleges and universities get," Hamilton said. "So that's a strike against us right away. Our alumni have been generous, but not at the levels needed for sustaining the college."

Less than a quarter of the college's $3.3 million annual budget comes from student fees and tuition, in part because the school remains smaller in enrollment. Additionally, the students and their families often lack the financial means to pay higher rates. As a result, the college needs to bring in more than half (57 percent) of its annual budget through donations just to keep the doors open.

"So about $1.7 million this year needs to show up from people and churches writing a check from Red Oak, Iowa, or from Chicago, from a Covenant Living residence facility, or right here in Alaska," Hamilton said.

By coming and paying for room and board while they work on campus, by bringing donations to help buy materials, the volunteers help supplement the college's income. And because those volunteers often end up giving to the college long after they have gone back to their homes, they fill the role that alumni donors play for other colleges.

Like many other colleges, ACC has also brought in revenue by renting out space to groups and conferences during the summers, when students are back home and there are empty beds in the school's halls, as well as in the three nearby apartment units the college has acquired over the years. By having local churches, student groups, mission agencies, or tourists stay on campus during the summer, the college can generate income needed for the mission.

"One of the ways that we have been able to scrape together some revenue in the summertime is through the rentals that we do on campus," said Hamilton.

The college has also developed relationships with foundations and with congregations who have become faithful supporters over the years. Those donors have included the M.J. Murdock Trust, whose support helped to launch the college and who has helped sustain the school over the years, and the Rasmuson Foundation, which was founded in the 1950s by the family of Olson and Edward Anton "E.A." Rasmuson. They had been Covenant missionary teachers in the village of Yakutat, and is the family who helped build the National Bank of Alaska. More than 100 congregations have also supported the college with their giving, as have nearly 2,000 individual donors annually over the years. It has truly taken a village to raise up the ministry of Alaska Christian College since 2000.

Epilogue

2 5 years. This journey has been the most adventurous of my life!
We have seen the incredible miracles of Jesus throughout our short history. God's people from rural Alaska to the southern tip of Florida and everywhere between have rallied since day one to meet our mission and vision. "Whole-life Discipleship" and "Life-changing Education" have been our passion as we have sought to "Empower Alaska Natives through biblically-based higher education and Christian formation to pursue excellence in character, learning, and service as followers of Christ." These are not just aspirations, they are the reality of what we have discovered to be our DNA as over 900 students have walked through our doors since that first day on Sept. 16, 2001 when we dedicated this college to the Lord Jesus Christ.

The Miracle on Royal Place story is not over. It would be easy to say that together we have accomplished what we set out to do 25 years ago and then rest on our status quo. It is so easy to move to "maintenance" mode after 25 years and manage what we have. Looking back is tremendously helpful as we have learned so much together about educating our Indigenous (and other) students who have made all the years possible. Looking back through our times of testing and making mistakes as a college have brought us wisdom that can't be read about in a book. Telling our old stories are exciting and remind us of God's faithfulness and provision. Hearing of changed lives for Jesus propelled us forward in our previous years and is why we are determined to do all that we do to serve these amazing students. With 30 acres and 28 different building projects that are completed and DEBT FREE should signify we can slow down now and pause on moving the mission forward. Even with a growing legacy endowment that had a great start since our earliest days doesn't mean we can stop securing the future of ACC's financial stability. God has shown up in both our times of living on the mountain top and when we have been in the darkest valley. Now is not the time to rely on and rest in our past, but to decide together to move ahead with clarity and our communal solid mission for the next 25 years and beyond.

I have but one hope for the future of ACC. It is simply this: to fulfill the great commission of Jesus by bringing the Indigenous nations to a saving relationship with Jesus through our chosen vehicle—Christian higher education.

Many have asked me over the years what drives ACC forward and I have consistently stated that it is to offer the opportunity for the student to make a decision about a relationship they can have with the Savior Jesus, to be formed through the lens of Scripture and education, to receive Christian counseling support through New Hope Counseling Center for their past wounds and hurts, and receive an accredited degree to move them to another college or a workforce opportunity they would simply not have without their degree in hand. Our graduates have made a mark in Alaska as they have started a relationship with Jesus and have carried that relationship with them where they serve in churches, native corporations, schools, tribal government, medical facilities, the military, village businesses, and hundreds of other jobs/experiences. When our students meet Jesus and receive Him, followed by discipleship/formation, they can change a village and a family. The great commission is being met with many of the students who have inculcated the mission of ACC and I am a humbled as a president because of how I have seen transformation of lives through what ACC offers to any student, from any background, any faith, any education, and any past, to join us with our open arms.

So, I have to look ahead. I have to look forward to what the Lord may want ACC to accomplish to serve the next generation of Alaska Indigenous (and other) young people. Our team will not sit and wait for the next set of miracles without the prayer and guidance of the Holy Spirit and with the passion we led with in our first 25 years. Our future is unknown and we don't know what the future holds, but as the hymn states, "we know Who holds our future."

During the 25th year, ACC is evaluating ourselves against the standards established by our accrediting agency. We are required to meet each of the nine accreditation standards and through self-examination of *everything* about ACC, we will end with a new strategic plan to propel us forward. At the writing of this book, the agency's evaluation is less than a half-year away, but we are working hard to examine ourselves to make our college excel in the years to come. I cannot state what will come out of this year-long process today, but a few strategic goals for our future are rising to the top.

First, ACC believes its "sweet spot" is a student body of approximately 75 students. This is a very sustainable number of students for ministry purposes, financial realities, and the facilities and staff we have to serve that student body. We endeavor to reach more students, beyond 2025, to reach this goal.

Second, ACC is poised to offer a curriculum that we believe best meets the educational needs of our Indigenous students. This means the expansion of career technical programs not previously offered. In 2024, ACC piloted our first courses in outboard motors and we are desiring to expand into other career technical offerings as funds are available. In addition, ACC needs to evaluate the current programs and courses that we have taught during the past decade or so, to best serve our students.

Third, in the coming years, ACC must consider diversifying our student body to invite many other students beyond only Alaska Indigenous students. ACC has been incredibly blessed to have had dozens of lower 48 Native American students attend and graduate from ACC since our inception and we wish to expand that population. We also have many Alaskans who may not be Indigenous but could greatly benefit from attending Alaska's only faith-based college for Indigenous students. This is not mission drift; it is fulfilling our mission by adding to our student body others who will join our Indigenous-priority college that has never shifted in its primary mission since day one.

Last, in the coming years, ACC could consider a relationship with Alaska Native high schoolers who could greatly benefit from receiving a Christian secondary education on the campus of ACC, of course with their own facilities, to reach a generation for Christ not currently being reached. There is no Christian high school in the state that, like ACC, reaches predominantly Indigenous Alaskans. Perhaps the Lord would give ACC the vision to begin the mission of educating younger

Alaskans as Covenant High School in Unalakleet did for 30 plus years, but closed in 1985. A dream? A potential ministry opportunity? Not a needed model anymore? Impractical? These questions would need to be answered for any future possibilities of "Alaska Christian Academy" becoming reality. Pray with me regarding this dream.

Our future is bright as many signs of our thriving as a college are right in front of us. We have had, and continue to have, an amazingly talented and gifted staff and faculty. Many of our students are hungry for the things of Christ and the community we have to offer. Our facilities are among the state's best for colleges our size. Our partnership with New Hope Counseling Center is solid with our students continuing to receive free counseling services from that dedicated team. The reputation of our college both locally and statewide is positive with those who best know us and how we serve these amazing students who many times, also teach us.

My deepest thanks to ACC's long-serving vice presidential team- Dr. Jeff Siemers, Executive Vice President and Provost (24 years), Rev. Sean Hoffbeck (18 years), and Eric Johnson (12 years), for their loyalty to the mission of ACC, their iron-sharpening our team, and abiding friendship through their 54 years of combined service at ACC. They have sacrificed, stood in the gap, and led with integrity. ACC would have not become what it is today apart from their deep sense of call to serve these amazing students in Jesus' name. I am grateful we've had all these years to do life together.

ACC has a sustainable model for its current population with the hopes, again, of increasing to our sweet spot of 75 students. We are financially sound with no debt. Our denomination, conference, and many other great churches continue to show their loyalty to the mission through their gifts and talented volunteers showing up each summer and during the academic year to serve the students and programs. We are thriving because we believe we have a BIG God who loves our students more than we do, and He wants a place of grace for these students to call home for the years they are with us. ACC is ready for the next 25 years and beyond because of the army of individuals, churches, foundations, corporations, and businesses who believe in Christian higher education, especially for the Indigenous population God has called us to specifically serve.

I must ask each of you, who have read this book to its end, these very important questions. Many of you have been on this adventurous and miraculous journey with us for all or part of our history. Many of you are co-owners of this mission and all that it entails. The Alaska Conference of the Evangelical Covenant Church may be the Member of ACC, but it is truly the thousands of friends of ACC who are members of ACC's immediate family and own this college on Royal Place.

My first question is this: how loyal have you been and can you continue to be for the future of ACC in the next 25 years and beyond? What lengths will you go to see ACC continue to thrive? Have you considered what your connection with ACC will be in the future and are you committed to sacrifice whatever is needed to bring the hope of Jesus and a Christian higher education experience to every student who walks through our doors? Are you willing to stand with ACC no matter what valleys and mountains may come in our future? I invite you to consider your place today in ACC's future history. I invite you to pray for each request you have read about in this book. I invite you to add ACC to your will, bequests, and legacy giving for our long-term sustainability. I ask you to invite students to consider ACC for their future educational endeavors. I invite you to show up on campus to serve in whatever capacity you may be able to offer of your time and talent. I invite you to join the ACC team permanently on our staff. Finally, I invite you to pray now for my successor as I cannot serve as president the next 25 years!

Gratitude is the word that best fits my heart and soul today as I close out this book. I am grateful for the Alaska Native elders and others that sought to fulfill this vision written about in these pages. I am grateful for the dozens of team members who have joined me in the first 25 years. You have served with passion for every student. I am grateful for every gift that arrives into our bank account through the sacrificial giving of thousands of you giving thousands of dollars for Life-Changing Education. I am grateful for our volunteers who have built this beautiful campus to the glory of God. I am grateful for each student that has taught me how to understand their culture and the strength and resilience in each one that has been a model to me. I am grateful for a spouse and three adult children who saw their husband/Dad infrequently in the early years and still love me today! Finally, I am grateful for Jesus who saved me from my sinful ways when I was 16 years old at a Covenant camp. That time has formed my life like nothing else over these past decades of being a follower of Jesus. He has been my "True North Guide" and best friend through thick and thin, hearing every prayer, and answering them according to His will. He has led us all in this great adventure. "To God be the glory, great things He has done."

My Dad wasn't a man of many words growing up, but I remember something he once said when I was a child after a camping trip. He said, "Son, always leave the campground cleaner than you found it." My best prayer is that, only by the grace of God, together we have left God's imprint on Alaska and its students, and our college is a little cleaner than we found it. I stand with Paul's words to the Philippians in Chapter 1, verse 6: "being confident of this, that He who began a good work in you will carry it on to completion until the day of Christ Jesus." May it be so.

Quyana, Taikuu, Thank you.

Rev. Dr. Keith J. Hamilton (or just Keith)

Alaska Christian College

35109 **Royal Place**, Soldotna, AK 99669

July 18, 2025

All proceeds from the sale of this book go to Alaska Christian College.

Appendices

These lists are possibly incomplete. We apologize in advance if a name has not been listed. If anyone knows of additional names that should be added, please contact ACC so that we can include them in future publications.

Student Alumni of the Year
(Board of Trustee Selection)
Adam London 2008
Donald Fancher 2009
Valerie Thomas 2009
Jimmy Andrew 2010
Kimberly Kakakaway 2011
Louisa (Jones) Hostetter 2012
Jon Taylor 2013
Shirleen (Wong) London 2014
Jason Battiest 2015
Darren Whitworth 2016
Melanie Shavings 2017
Doris (Hugo) Shavings 2018
Adrianne Woody 2019
Jaber Mohamed 2021
Sylvia (Sheldon) Fancher 2022
Beatrice (Olrun) Kiokun 2023
Allysia Smith 2024
Brenda (Dock) Hagen 2025

Students of the Year
2002
Adam London
Lucinda Benally

2003
Jason Battiest
Valerie Thomas

2004
Ryan Mute
Charis Sheldon
Beatrice Katongan

2005
Louisa Jones
Cameron Mixsooke

2006
Cheryl Johnson
Blassi Shoogukwruk

2007
Kelly Walton
Darren Whitworth

2008
John "Lupi" Anaver
Stephanie Olrun

2009
Matt Blair
Janelle Richards

2010
Aaron Towarak
Melanie Shavings

2011
Jaber Mohamed
Brenda Dock

2012
Brenda Evak
Vincent Schaeffer

2013
Phillip Kopanuk
Brandi Moore

2014
Levi Brink
Kaylin Kopp

2015
Levi Brink
Brandi Moore

2016
Jennie Powers
Justus Eben

2017
Justus Eben
Jessica Murran

2018
Charis Ivanoff
Alex Tsakos

2019
Talakai Finau
Makayla Kameroff

2020
Chris Adams
Makayla Kameroff

2021
Michael George
Marilyn Moore

2022
William Beaver
Buff Brink

2023
Justina Peterson
Walter Bell

2024
Naomi Snyder
Vernon "Ace" Coffin

2025
Catherine Prisk
Dennis Pete

Original Staff, July 1, 2001
Keith and Debbie Hamilton
Curtis and Kristi Ivanoff
Mark and Joanna Hill
Alan and Sharon Finifrock
Bob and Phyllis Mickelson
Jeff Siemers
Eva (Oyoumick) Harrell

Additional Fall/Spring Staff, 2001-2002
Ira Isaac
Steve and Bev McKinley
Dorcas Layman
Claire and Clara Schnupp
Rev. Scott Pitsch
Dr. Cheryl Davis (Siemers)
Rev. Dan Thornton
Rev. Dave Dahms
Rev. Paul Wilson
David and Carolyn Alexander
Jim Engwall
Craig Warzeha
Bob Bode
Kisha Ballot
Carlie McCahn
Judy Swanson
Janice Thornton
Silviu Hofman
Jack and Nancy Phelps

Original ACC Task Force Members
Rob Hall
Paul Wilson
Byron Bruckner
John Hege
Steve Peterson
Joel Caldwell
Neil Josephson
Sandy Gold
Mark Hill
Trevor Simpson
Curtis Ivanoff

Jon Payne
Barbara Johnson
Nancy Hjelm
Keith Hamilton
Eva Oyoumick
Jeff Siemers

Alaska Leadership College Members
Jeff Siemers, Staff
Students
Tom Mute
Byron Moses
Doug Swanson
Alyona Natwick
Elia Gomez
Ruth Noratuk

First Board of Directors
Keith Hamilton
Paul Wilson
Jon Payne
Nancy Hjelm
Trevor Simpson
Steve Hostetter
Nathan Nagaruk
Barbara Johnson
Joel Caldwell
Jerry Daniels
Doc Nicholson
Advisory: Rob Hall, John Hege, Byron Bruckner, Neil Josephson

Legacy Volunteers
(Significant Time Spent Serving on Campus)

Dennis and Connie Schnicke, Larry Streiff, Bob and Phyllis Mickelson, Silviu Hofmann, Craig Warzeha, Laura Hofmann, Dennis and Mary Carlson, Tim Amundsen, Dick Nelson, Jim Ramsey, Bob Bode, Al and Judy Nelson, Ike Dotomain, Willie and Von VanDorp, Rick and Pat Adams, Roger and Caryn Rosengren, Richard Borgeson, Mary Beth Johnson, Gary and Susan Palmer, Dan and Terri Franklin, Stan Wells, Eleanor Butler, Glen and Millie Mehrkens, Alan and Sharon Finifrock, Marv and Jan Eppard, Jay and Sandy Rupp, Arlyn and Denise Mund, Lee Bolger, David and Dottie House, David Wainscott, Gloria Tamte, Owen and Linda Deckinga, Harvey and Linda Lundquist, Rollin Gust, Jack Renick, Paul Swanson, Dale Solberg, Lois Link Solberg, Debbie Sonberg, Willie Brendon, Marjory Wiley, Larry and Carolyn Seilhamer, Gary and Sharon Williams, Kathy Caddy, Motoy Nakumara, John Tissell, Irene Houdek, Adam London, Jon Murphy, Jason Battiest, Steve Johnson, Andy Beauchamp, Mark and Bev Arnold, Roy and Carol Nachtigal, Chuck Ford, Joanna Hill, Beth Sandell, Lisa Glynn Peterson, Jim Nelson, Gary and Louise Hicks, Dan Nielsen, Dan Lewis, Charles Johnson, Nathanael Putnam, Larry and Blanche Krumm, Don Hjelle, Grace Buckner, Luke Oliver, Keith DeRousse, Ralph and Ruthie Carlson, Helen Gulledge, Lynn and Rachel Farley, Jim Milton, Shannon Hoffbeck, Mike and Gloriann Kramer, Gary Cardinale, Peggy and Mike Nystrom, Kristi Ivanoff, Josh Shipley, Jill Scharold, the Prayer Team of Sandy Gold, Judy Cook and Heather Smith, and a host of other saints who have volunteered over the years for long stretches of time. They have been the backbone of the volunteer effort to build both ACC's programs and buildings. Their legacy will continue into eternity.

Church Volunteer Work Teams (Sowers)

Arvada Covenant, CO 2001/02/03/04/05/06/07/08/09/10/11/12/13/14/16/17/19
/21/22/23/24/25

Community Covenant, Lenexa, KS- 2001/02/03/04/05/06/12/14/15/16/17

Castle Oaks Covenant, Castle Rock, CO -2001

Clairemont Covenant, San Diego, CA -2001

Moose Lake Covenant, MN -2001/02

N. Mankato/Crossview Covenant, MN -2002/03/04/05

First Covenant Church, Iron Mountain, MI -2002

Roseville Covenant, MN -2002/08/10

First Covenant, Grand Rapids, MI -2002

Hillside Covenant, Walnut Creek, CA -2002/04/06/08/16/18

First Covenant, Red Wing, MN- 2002/03/04/05/06/16/17/18/19/21/25

Cutler Baptist, ME -2003/05/17

First Covenant, Rockford, IL- 2003/04/05/06/07/08/09/10/17

Rockford Area Churches, IL- 2022/23/24/25

Bethany Covenant, Berlin, CT -2010/24

Faith in Action, Appleton, WI -2003/05/17

Forest Park Covenant, Muskegon, MI -2003/04/05/06/07/08/09/10/17/18/22/25

Alexandria Covenant, MN -2003/05/06/08/17/18/19/21/22/23/25

Easton Covenant, CT -2003/17

Cedarville University, OH -2003

Sanctuary Covenant, Sacramento, CA -2003

First Covenant, Willmar, MN -2004/14/17/25

Cornerstone Covenant, Turlock, CA -2004

First Covenant, Oakland, CA-2004/05/06/07/08/09

Hinsdale Covenant, IL -2004/09/19/22

Zion Covenant, Jamestown, NY -2004/06

Salem Covenant, New Brighton, MN -2005/06/17/18/21/23/24/25

Faith Covenant, Burnsville, MN -2005/06

Escalon Covenant, CA -2005/06/07/08/09/10/11/12/13/14/15/16/17/18/19/21/22

Plymouth Covenant, MN -2006/11/12/13/14/15/16/17/18/19/21/22/23/24/25

Pine Lake Covenant, Sammamish, WA -2006

Covenant Church, West Lafayette, IN -2006/07
Newport Covenant, Bellevue, WA -2008/09/17/19/22
Deerbrook Covenant, Lee's Summit, MO -2009
Lakeview Covenant, Duluth, MN -2009/10/12/14/16/17/18/19/21/22/23/24/25
Roseau Covenant, MN -2010
Dassel Covenant, MN -2010
Libertyville Covenant, Green Oaks, IL -2011
Redeemer Covenant, Brooklyn Park, MN -2011/17/19/21
Bear Track Bible Church, Beattyville, KY -2012
Crossroads Covenant, Ft. Collins, CO -2012
Christian Outreach, AZ -2014
North Coast Community Church, Vista, CA -2014
Rolling Hills Covenant Church, Rolling Hills Estates, CA -2015/17/18/19/20/21/22/23/24/25
McMinnville Covenant, OR -2016/23
Flatirons Community Church/Mund Family, CO -2016/17/18/19/20/21/22/23/24/25
Simi Valley Covenant, CA -2017/25
Broadway Covenant, Rockford, IL -2017/21
Community Covenant, Rocklin, CA -2016/17/18/19/21/22/23/24/25
Lakeview Covenant, Tarpon Springs, FL -2017
Seeds of Hope/Safety Harbor Covenant, FL -2017/18/19/21/22/23/24/25
Bridges Covenant, Tavares, FL -2017
Shoreline Covenant, WA -2018/23
Modesto Covenant, CA -2018/19/22/23/24/25
Fireplace Fellowship, PA-2018
Cousins for Christ, KY-2016/17/18/21/23
Sapphire Homes, Bellevue, WA -2019
Sunset Presbyterian Church, Portland, OR -2019/21/22/23
He's Alive Church, Kannapolis, NC -2019/20/21/22/23/24/25
Life Community Covenant, Roseville CA -2019/21
Westwood Presbyterian Church, Wichita, KS -2021/22/23
Bayside Covenant, Granite Bay, CA -2023/24/25

Judson Baptist Church, Brentwood, TN -2024/25
Bethany Covenant, Mt. Vernon, WA 2025

Charter Churches (Initial Major Gifts to Start ACC)
Arvada Covenant Church, CO
First Covenant Church, Portland, OR
First Covenant Church, Iron Mountain, MI
North Mankato/Crossview Covenant Church, MN
Community Covenant Church, Shawnee/Lenexa, KS
First Covenant Church, Red Wing, MN
First Covenant Church, Rockford, IL
Forest Park Covenant Church, Muskegon, MI
First Covenant Church Oakland, CA
Hinsdale Covenant, IL
Faith Christian Community Church, Anchorage, AK
First Covenant Church, Willmar, MN
Hillside Covenant Church, Walnut Creek, CA
Zion Covenant Church, Jamestown, NY
All Saints Episcopal Church, Anchorage, AK
Community Covenant Church, Eagle River, AK
Changepoint Church, Anchorage, AK

Charter Members (Initial Major Gifts to Start ACC)
Griffey, Ralph and Gunny
Holmgren, Kathy and Mike
Sauer, Deb and Dean
Ideker, Doug and Terrie
Anderson, Chris and Julie
Robblee, Andy and Michelle
Blankmeyer, Jon and Elaine
Gorin, John and Vicky
Lundell, LeRoy and Pearl
Reese, Randy and Jane
Robblee, David and Anne

Persons, Bill and Jan
Oehlerich, Marjorie
Larsen, David and Betty
Helwig, David and Nancy
Eikenberry, Roger and Jan

"Ten-year" (tenure) Award Recipients
(Volunteers With 10 Years of Summer Service)
Arlyn and Denise Mund
Jack Renick
Jill Scharold
Keith Jackson
John and Becky Ihne
Roger and Caryn Rosengren
Rollin Gust
Richard Borgeson
Rick Adams
David and Dottie House
Chuck Ford
Michael Ford
Paul Funk
Gary and Susan Palmer
Jim and Laurie Arndt
Scott Zimmerman
Al and Sharon Finifrock
William and Von VanDorp
Marion Van Vliet
Saundra Miller
Mark and Bev Arnold
Dan Lewis
Dan and Terri Franklin

Team Nehemiah Members
(Maintenance Volunteers Serving During the Academic Year and Summer
for Six Weeks or More)
Dan Franklin
Ike Dotomain
Chuck Ford
Lee Bolger
Tim Amundsen
Arlyn Mund
Jack Renick
Rick Adams
Steve Johnson
Mary Beth Johnson
Dennis and Mary Carlson
David House
Mark and Bev Arnold
Mike Kramer
Harvey Lundquist